THE BONUS ROUND

CORPORATE SALES

LESSONS & STRATEGY

Patrick Tinney

2020

First Printing: 2020

ISBN 978-0-9938284-7-8

Centroid Publishing

STN Main, 150 King Street P.O. Box 713

Peterborough, Ontario, Canada K9J 6Z8

www.centroidmarketing.com

Ordering Information:

Special discounts are available on quantity purchases by corporations, associations, educators, and others. For details, contact the publisher at the above listed address.

U.S. trade bookstores and wholesalers: Please contact

Centroid Publishing Tel: 1-705-657-2518

Email: patrick@centroidmarketing.com

DEDICATION

Steven J. Cosic.

Steve was a dear friend, golf partner, business guru, media buying professional, real estate investor, and negotiation super-power.

Stevo left the corporate world at just the right moment and, somehow, he knew it. I am blessed to have known him. Steve owned the term, ***The Bonus Round***, with his theatrical closure of monster media deals. Anyone who sat across a negotiation table from Steve was invited to watch a bargaining savant, painting works of art. Steve lived ***The Bonus Round***.

CONTENTS

INTRODUCTION

If you are reading *The Bonus Round Corporate Sales Lessons & Strategy*, you are either a corporate sales warrior or you are interested in leveling-up to corporate sales. If you miss corporate selling because it was so much fun, this may also be a reason you are reading this book. From 1980 to 2007, I was in corporate sales in one form or another. My chosen field of sales was in the media business, selling daily and community newspaper products. I sold to the vast majority of North America's largest retailers and advertising agencies. Big money was at play. Anytime big money is at play, there is enormous opportunity.

The truth is that if you are average in the corporate sales world, the only thing that can save you is a sellers' market where there are too many buyers of a product and not enough sellers. This is how corporate sales operated from about 1950 to 2000. After this period, the Internet and social media changed everything. From about 2000 and onward, anyone in any part of the world could compete with you without you even knowing. We must all be prepared for intense competition and change because it is inevitable.

I just loved my time in corporate sales. It was huge fun, exciting, and even breathtaking at times. I was selling across every time zone in Canada, and I could not get enough of it. The companies that I worked for were open to new ideas around how products were packaged and incentivized for large customers. This just made my chili boil. I relished the idea of being able to help gigantic customers in creative ways, while helping my company's stakeholders hit their objectives and targets. The speed and urgency were mind boggling. It was just crazy, insane- rip-the-skin-off-the-ball fun!

For me, working in corporate sales for the **Toronto *Star***, the Southam Newspaper Group, Hollinger Inc., and CanWest Media was like playing for the New York Yankees every day. I am not a huge baseball fan, but I would visualize what it was like to walk on to the Yankees' baseball field. It is a bold, powerful, and enlightened feeling. It made me tingle a bit. That is corporate sales at its finest.

To put my corporate sales life in context, here are a few short numbers.

In 1996, I signed the largest FSI (free standing insert) contract in our company's history. It was a jumbo sale at $4 Million annually with Zellers department stores. That contract rolled over for the next 15 years without many changes, meaning that over its lifetime it was a $40+ Million sale. Zellers was sold to Target Corporation in 2011.

Contracts with these large accounts were generally signed with one signature mine and the customer. In those days, we did not have committees signing contracts. Ponder this, if money doubles in value every 7 to 10 years, just imagine the value of those contracts in today's dollars?

I hope that as you read **The Bonus Round**, you will take some ideas from these pages and reshape them to work for you on your corporate sales mission. Ideas never get old. Ideas are our true north. Integrity is our true north. Thinking with a fertile mind is true north. Having grit and guts are our true north. I hope you enjoy your reading of **The Bonus Round**. Now, let's unpack some ideas and lessons that will help you sell to whale-sized accounts. We are talking Yankee Stadium whale-sized accounts. Let's giddy up!

Tip: Go out of your way to know your customers and their competitors as well or better than they do. In my first two books, ***Unlocking Yes, the Revised Edition*** and ***Perpetual Hunger***, I refer to this as reconnaissance.

Recon is your responsibility and a must. If you don't think like a corporate customer insider, you will be treated as a commoditized outsider.

Patrick Tinney

PART I – PHILOSOPHY

1

MY CORPORATE CONSULTATIVE SELLING PHILOSOPHY

If you have read my two sales books, *Perpetual Hunger* and *Unlocking Yes, the Revised Edition*, you'll know that I buried a philosophy for sales prospecting and sales negotiation in each of these books. My belief as the Founder of Centroid Sales Training is that if a sales professional does not have a hierarchical base to stand on regarding prospecting and negotiation, they have nothing to fall back on. Sales professionals need a base to return to when they get stumped by buyers who are confusing them.

The same goes for corporate consultative selling. If you do not have a mission, you end up with a wobbly cause, in my view. With this in mind, let me share my philosophy and hierarchical view of consultative selling.

1)   **When customers speak, we listen.** Honestly, listening is the Mt. Everest of consultative selling, yet many in sales still struggle with listen-

ing. If you are going to be a successful consultative corporate seller, you have to train yourself to stop jumping over customers in conversation. If the customer is just about to hand you the keys to their building, you should just stop, pause, and listen. Let the customer finish. Be contemplative. Acknowledge their concerns, needs, and aspirations. Selling is not about us. It is about how he/she buys.

2)   **Relationships build trust.** I share with my Centroid Sales Training participants that, "If you do not have a bridge to your customer, you had better enjoy swimming." Trust takes weeks, months, and sometimes years to build, but only takes two seconds to dismantle. Your words, actions, and inactions speak volumes to buyers in "whale-sized corporations." Please remember: as sales professionals, we are all walking and talking brands/promises. Keep your promises and build trusted relationships that may well evolve into lifetime friendships.

3)   **Succeed with deeds.** When in a situation where I am dealing with a new contact in a corporate setting, I am always aware that someone has to start to build the relationship. I want that someone to be me. The way that I start building trust is to offer meaningful value to my corporate customer in our early engagements. The deed could be sharing some research that they do not have access to or may not be aware of. It could be showing them how we help other customers in similar verticals with a demonstration or a test. These are low self-interest, low risk, value building deeds that the customer will recognize immediately. You can do this. Succeed with deeds and extend the olive branch. Dream customers are out there. You just have to find them.

4)   **Anticipate needs.** If you really want to get a buyer's attention in the corporate world, get ahead of their planning curve. If you spend a little time with them and ask the right kinds of exploratory and qualifying questions, they may share their vision of the future. They may even share the gap that exists between where their company is now in relation to where they want

to be in the future. As a corporate seller, if I can identify these customer aspirational need gaps, I want to fill them. This can happen by researching what the customer's competitors are doing to gain an advantage. It could be data matched with mapping to build a visual picture. It could be a new way of understanding how they can address their new target customers. Work on this and you will be seen as an insider in your corporate customer's world.

5)	**We all win.** When transparent, collaborative planning is shared with a customer, they will love you for it. It means that you have their most profound interests at heart and you are willing to share with them so all can prosper and profit. The term "win/win" comes to mind. I like the term "everyone wins." It is powerful when everyone pulls in the same direction so both of our businesses grow while continuing to explore and collaborate as one spirit.

Lessons Learned. Trust is earned; no one owes anyone trust. Words and deeds matter. Actions speak louder than words. There is amazing power in collective thinking and experimentation. None of us are smarter than all of us. Seek to be seen as a trusted insider in your customer's building. You will know you are there when special invitations to listen to delicate information come your way. Show respect. Be the professional that they trust to invite to their business party. Consultative selling is such an amazing experience, especially when there is a lot on the line and your customer knows you will show up.

2

CORPORATE SALES IS PANORAMIC

In the world of corporate sales, larger ticket products and services have a longer sales cycle. Today, we face even more obstacles because we are living in a buyer's market with too many sellers and not enough buyers. This slows the sales cycle down even more. Notwithstanding, I am very optimistic about corporate sales and its four vistas bolted together to complete a bold, brilliant, and strong sales panorama. In corporate sales… plan for the bonus round.

1)   **Sales Prospecting**.

In a local market, a seller should expect several competitors for a product or service being sold. With the corporate job market tightening, there has been an increase in entrepreneurs that will keep local sellers on their toes more than ever. Local markets must be cut, brushed, combed, and scraped for every last tidbit of possible customer expenditure. The free rides and massive expansion of yesteryear are few and far between locally. This means that local sellers must wake up every morning starving or have someone else eat their breakfast.

In the corporate world, as fresh, new expenditure money starts to percolate in the bowels of the professional buying world, sellers will smell this aroma. Where fresh, new active money is concerned, everything leaks. A whiff of new money travels fast to regions far and wide. This whiff creates a "bees on honey" sensation that drives sellers out of their dens with perpetual hunger. As corporate sellers know, we must do as much homework as possible on new active money. We must uncover deep, unique customer needs well before making first contact with this new active account. Corporate sellers must build a solid business case to secure a much-needed buyer appointment displaying deep and meaningful seller value. We must have the sense of an insider before we exchange that first "I am listening" salutation with a buyer who is wise and steely. These corporate buyers know that once the word is out, that fresh money is in play, there will be nowhere to hide. Corporate, perpetual hunger operates 24/7 globally and does not need rest. Even when global corporate sellers decide to rest, we let our computers do the perpetual hunting for us. This is the world of corporate sales prospecting. It exemplifies "perpetual hunger." This is the left side of the corporate sales panoramic view. Make no mistake, though, hunters will enter this selling picture from all sides.

2)   **Consultative Selling**.

Rather than drowning our buyer partner with data, we have conversations. We meet and break bread with our friend, when they have an opening. It's all about their world. It's about how our friend sees the future and the gaps that they query us about. Our friend lets us know that in an emergency, we are her/his first call and vice/versa. We look for ways to help each other achieve collaborative goals, where both sides take a little risk. We do this to make the kinds of business gains that are meaningful to peers and superiors in both of our worlds. There is buying and selling; it is continuous. We fix problems before they become issues. We have each other's best interests at heart. It is consultative selling, but it's bigger. It is more of a forward-looking symbiotic relationship.

3)   **Sales Negotiation.**

Every company has its needs/wants list when it comes to corporate negotiations. The money is big, and it is serious. We are friends with our buyer partners. We both know that our bonus payouts depend on how we represent our respective companies and its stakeholders. After a quarter or a year of executing with great precision, it is now time for "The Bonus Round." Our buyer partner may be opening in new markets. She/he needs our cooperation, support, and creativity to achieve an edge on the market. We are being asked to step up with great incentive plans to justify new and robust buyer expenditures. There may be some tough news from the buying side as well. Strategic plans change. Old ideas have had their day and their budget. It is time to let the old ideas rest for a while because new exciting ideas are at the fore. Our buyer friend is looking for our commitment to help him/her make new strategies happen in real time.

Our side has created an eye-popping set of proposals for our buyer that will not only meet, but also exceed last year's performance. We need to grow in stride with our buyer partner. There are markets that we want to acquire from our competitors in a way that decreases the risks for us and for our buyer partner. It will be a seamless conversion. We will back test and we will be there to live up to all of our brand promises. The selling side needs a couple of extra wins since we worked hard for every dollar this year. There is a need not only to feed our troops, but to bring more business on our side. Nevertheless, we stride forward with our buyer partner. It is mental chess and the pre-meetings can be a bit testy. The takes and puts are fair, but they're not all we had hoped for. Notwithstanding, we will exceed budget when our buyer partner signs the contract. When big money is on the line, it is not a noisy, lumpy affair. There is usually no yelling, but there may be some strong words. Straight talk is what commitments are all about. It is "The Bonus Round."

4)   **Delivery/Payment**.

Everyone needs to be fulfilled by what they bought and sold. No corporate sales year is complete without payment and reconciliation. This is how corporate buyer and seller professionals navigate, manage, and look to the future while reliving past victories. This is corporate partnership at its best. Everyone stretches out a hand. Neither partner can do this alone in the year ahead.

Lessons Learned. It takes very skilled people to buy and sell at the corporate level. These are professionals who already are or are about to be best of breed. Remember, great friends are hard to find, so treat them as family. We are all in this together. This is what "The Bonus Round" is all about.

3

THE PROFESSIONAL YOU

The professional (pro) you in corporate sales is not necessarily about you, the personal brand. The pro you gets painted a little differently. The pro you stands out in an environment of sameness that can often happen in a corporate sales setting, where culture can at times drink up all of the oxygen in the building.

The pro you means that if your colleagues close their eyes, they know you are there. Notwithstanding, let's unpack how the pro you gets noticed and is remarkable.

1)   **Attire**

A long-time friend and colleague, Xavier, has always had a great sense of cool with the way he wraps himself in clothing. Xavier can be wearing a suit or a shirt that he has owned for years and, yet, he always looks fresh and well kept. He looks great in just about everything he wears, but it is the way he carries himself that I have always admired. The same goes for another old friend, Randy. Dress Randy up in a T-shirt and a leather jacket and he can attend just about any function. Randy carries himself so well and is always groomed to the teeth. In a corporate setting, many are simply trying to look like they didn't just crawl out of bed. Not these two gents. Note to self: how are you draping yourself for customer engagements and those around you? It matters.

2)   Self-Awareness

I love a great cigar about once or twice a year, but I would not want to sit beside someone who smokes them constantly. The same goes for people who shower in aftershave. I know it sounds petty, but customers and colleagues notice.

3)   Time

Some sales professionals are so aware of time that they are never late and never hold a meeting up. They just manage their time so well that they are rarely the last person in the door for customer or internal meetings. This matters in the corporate world. If you get a reputation for constantly being late, important customers will notice and take it as a big-time slight.

4)   Office Space

I have always tried to keep my personal space at work in reasonable shape. I was never Mr. Clean, but always aware. I have seen some workspaces that look like battle fields that have been carpet bombed for weeks. If you cannot keep your workspace under control, you will lose or misplace important things. Your smart phone cannot hold everything. If your manager walks by and sees a battlefield on your desk week after week, one of two things goes through their head. This guy is so busy booking business, he cannot keep up. Or, this guy is out of control.

5) Noise

I have a deep, loud voice. At times, in an open office setting it did not serve me well. I was aware of it though. If I had long customer conversations that were jocular in nature because that was the way the customer liked it, I would book a small meeting room. I did not want to disturb those around me. Respect others.

6) Body Language

Some people are totally clueless when it comes to the body language they exhibit. This goes for both men and women. Make sure that what you are projecting is what you would want to see in others. To be blunt, would you buy from a person that exhibited your body language? I hope so.

7) Street Language

I grew up in Hamilton, Ontario, Canada. It was a steel town. If you live in the United States, think Pittsburgh or Allentown. Blue collar street slang permeated the city. When I started selling for a local newspaper in affluent Oakville, Ontario, I was pulled aside by my manager. He said, "Kid, drop the street slang. Speak like the sales professional we know you can be." He was very kind and the change in my language had an immediate, positive change in my sales results.

8) Shoe Shine

Back in my early days at the Toronto Star, I would walk around the office every day to see how many of my colleagues began their day. One of my younger peers, Steve, would start every day by shining his shoes so they gleamed. On the other hand, when I joined Southam Newspapers, we had a director of advertising from one of our eastern dailies who would roll into Toronto to make calls. His shoes looked like he had spent the night in a dumpster. Think about it. Whom would you emulate?

9)   Clothing Creativity

I have a successful business colleague who is colour blind. In his early days, dressing for work must have been a nightmare. He was creative though. He shopped at a great men's fashion store whose staff took great delight in numbering all of my colleague's clothing. No matter what the business setting, my colour-blind friend always looked like a finely turned out clothes horse.

10)   Dinner Etiquette

I have sat across the table from some very well-heeled businesspeople. I am amazed that their parents did not show them how to hold a knife and fork. Business dining should be a graceful event, not a dog fight. Some do not even know where to begin in a formal flatware table setting. If you are in business and are not food aware, take some etiquette training. It will pay dividends and you will not turn your customers off.

11)   Respect Others

As I often say to my son, "It takes a lifetime to become a gentleman. It takes two seconds to be the other thing."

12)   Humility

I earned the life I live by my own hand. I had a lot going against me as a young person. There was poverty, crime, alcohol abuse, and it gets worse. This teaches you that others down on their hands and knees probably did not choose the path they are on. Everyone deserves our kindness. Everyone deserves a second chance. What are you doing to perpetuate this thinking?

Lessons Learned. Selling is a craft. Treat your work as does a great artist or chess master. Have the best smile you can afford. Be the pro that is deep within you. Be the pro that sets the bar for those in your business. Remember, great customers seek great sales professionals.

4

CORPORATE ENGAGEMENT QUESTIONS MATTER

Planning questions for corporate, whale-sized customer engagements are critical. I use five sets of questions in these engagements. Here, I want to discuss the four most important. These questions can and must be ranked by dollar value in preparing for your corporate customer call and negotiation objectives. Please note that all four of the questions below are open ended and designed to induce lengthy, detailed replies from your corporate partners. These questions are about them, not us. They begin with "How", "What", "Why", "Where", "Who", "When", and "Which."

Exploratory Questions. When we first meet with a corporate customer, we want to know how they view their world and their industry. We want to understand their unique story and their vision of the future. Listening to their answers helps us gain a greater understanding of how we can help them solve present and future problems with exploratory questions such as these:

"What is a sales opportunity in your industry that you can see, but cannot not touch with your current resources?"

"Where do you see the most opportunity to take market share from your current competitors?"

"What customer base really means a lot to you now and into the future?"

"How do you see selling more products to your ideal customers now and in the future?"

Qualifying Questions. Where budgets, timing, quality, and resources are concerned, qualifying questions are time savers. Qualifying questions are the diamond standard. They help us clearly understand the corporate client's buying process, commitment, and most profound needs. Here are some useful and impactful qualifying questions:

"When do you want to launch this amazing new product?"

"What is your marketing budget for the launch?"

"Who in your organization makes the final decision on budget deployment?"

"What part of the country do you plan to start the rollout of this product launch?"

Trial Close Questions. Trial closes are created for decision-makers to close important deals. Trial closes are innocuous and really get to the heart of time, features, usage, place, and great future value to the customer. Ask trial close questions to elegantly close a sale. If you run out of time or have asked all the trial close questions you can, it may be time to just ask for the business. Here are some easy to remember trial close questions:

"How do you see this proposal moving forward?"

"What do you like most about this proposal?"

"Who in your company will benefit most from the implementation of this proposal?"

"When and where do you want to roll this proposal out?"

Causality Questions. The cool thing about causality questions is they beg the corporate customer to measure risk. Causality questions are big picture, looking into the future questions. These are super impactful questions, so use them more as a tactical rather than a strategic maneuver. Here are a couple of examples:

"How would you feel one month down the road that you could have saved thousands of dollars by implementing this proposal today rather than waiting?"

"What would your stakeholders think if they knew implementing this proposal today would avert costly risk in the near future?"

Lessons Learned. Professional corporate sellers are master detectives and master listeners. Professionals know that key client information may only pop up once in a giant customer engagement because the information is sensitive. Always take notes in these engagements and show maximum compassion and empathy. Practice your engagement questions. Rank them for dollar value impact. When in doubt, take a note-taker with you. Tagging your boss or coordinator to join you on a call as a note-taker is an all-pro move and will be observed by your corporate customers.

Book Recommendation. To raise your question efficacy and productivity even more, please read the following book: *DISCOVER Questions Get You Connected: For Professional Sellers* by Deb Calvert.

5

EMBRACING POSITIVE RISK IS A MINDSET

For as long as I can remember, I have been one of those persons who embraced positive risk. There was no choice. If you have read my story in my sales prospecting book, *Perpetual Hunger*, you know this started for me as a child out of profound loss and need.

There were times when I could take my positive risk gear and kick it up another notch. When in high school, I was bored and needed money. My attention turned to working, and heavy work at that. I delivered pianos for most of my high school years. At times, I was working 40 hours a week. Working this hard took pressure off of my mother. My mother put a roof over my head. I took care of the rest. If I wanted to go to college, I needed to find money because my family had no money to give me. The financial cupboards were bare.

When I finally found the Retail Advertising Program at Sheridan College in Oakville, Ontario, I embraced positive risk and totally owned it. I was hired full-time in the newspaper business while still in college. With a friend, I moved to Edmonton, Alberta from Hamilton, Ontario. Embracing positive risk entailed moving from one end of Canada to the other and back again twice because job opportunities in the newspaper business were everywhere. All I could see was positive risk and great ladders toward more lucrative sales roles.

By the time I was 29 years old, I was working for the largest newspaper group in Canada. I believe I was the second youngest person that the Southam Newspaper Group had hired at their corporate sales office in Toronto. You really have to be on your game to work in this kind of environment. This was big, serious money at play and I loved it.

Tons of positive risk opportunities were staring at me, but I could also see big blockages. For instance, during the first week I was on the job, I asked the manager of national sales what our negotiation perimeters were with large customers. In a blink, he told me to never negotiate. He followed up with, "Sell, that's your job." With that comment, I pulled out my desk dictionary in front of him and crossed out the word negotiation, I showed it to him. I am not sure he got my sense of disbelief.

Southam was taken over by Hollinger Newspapers and, in uncertain times, the doors swung wide open for me. The daily newspapers' Advertising VPs from across the company metro markets voted me in as "Sales leader" of the flyer distribution portfolio. My mission was to guide Hollinger's 125+-strong stable of newspapers into a new era. From that point on, I was launching products as often as I could. I did this as long as I could visualize a profit using all our production equipment and supplier printing equipment that I could harness.

The last product I launched took well over a year to develop and perfect. My patience, attention to detail, and thoroughness paid off. I launched a product called "Print, Plan, and Distribute", and the sales professionals in our corporate sales offices embraced it right away. Our sales professionals sold over $1 Million in unbudgeted, very profitable revenue in the first 2 quarters of the launch of this product. I was so proud of these sales professionals who embraced my positive risk and made it their own.

Rather than talk about all of the products I launched or had a hand in launching, I want to give you some pointers on how to get into this profound level of confident, positive risk yourself.

1)   Make sure you complete your industry education and do your best to specialize in a vertical within your industry. I cannot tell you how important this is. I was a distribution and production specialist. This is what set me apart from my sales and management peers.

2)   Learn how to conduct a SWOT (strengths, weaknesses, opportunities, threats) analysis on any product or service you plan to bring to market. This will guide you to the clearest truth about the viability of a product or service entering the market.

3)   Learn how to build a business case for a product. This learning takes time. Notwithstanding, the more you work at this business case exercise, the better you will become at it.

4)   Test your new product ideas with peers, management, and production. If your product will not work using your existing machinery, your company is going to have to invest. This is where new products get bogged down, or even die, owing to investment risk.

5)   The product test phase is where you should expect failures and lots of them. This is why it is called the test phase. Be fearless and keep working out the wrinkles. Don't rush. Test until you have made peace with your

product and not before. If it takes 50 or 100 tests to get it right, so be it. There's no right number. There is attention to detail and flawless execution.

6)   Don't rush products to market, regardless of the pressure others around you place on your shoulders. It is your career that is on the line. It is not theirs.

7)   Be sure you sell through to your sales peers. The very people you work with on the sales floor have the power to make or break a product launch. It is critical to make sure you give them all the training, marketing materials, and coaching they need to be successful.

8)   Be confident. Don't show any sign of weakness about a product launch. If you show any weakness, there will be a "stench in the air", and this will alert the sharks who might seek to block you.

9)   Have your customers' best interests at heart. If you focus on helping your customers make money, they will be interested and have your back. I cannot emphasize this enough. Customers love to be on the cutting edge of new product launches. They will support product launches as long as they know you and your company have done all of the testing to make a product launch bulletproof.

10)   Be your own best friend. It can get a little lonely out there on the edge. Be humble. Praise others for their work and dedication. Enjoy victories. Positive risk is for the brave.

Lessons Learned. Look for positive risk opportunities in your sales world and think about my 10 recommendations. Start thinking big. You can do it.

6

CORPORATE BUYERS ARE FINANCIAL GENIUSES

When you move into major account selling, you are going to be calling on the biggest businesses in your product category. You may even be calling on some of the biggest businesses in the world. It all sounds exciting and a bit ominous at the same time. After all, if you are contacting buyers who grew into these procurement positions, surely, they are fearless and make almost no mistakes. These buyers must be financial geniuses to keep all of their buying activities straight in their minds if they are purchasing for an entire country, continent, or even the world.

As a sales professional, it's true that you really must have your game on to call on these types of whale-sized accounts. Notwithstanding, let's have a chat about the buyers' super powers.

1)   **Buyers Are Fearless**. Not so, my sales professional friends. If anything, buyers are more cautious than most of us in sales. Buyers actually

have to take any sales proposals we present and repackage these recommendations internally for their corporate teams, regional, and even local stakeholders. Buyers do this to build a business case to be reviewed for value by their superiors. I am certain buyers have to do a ton of homework about you as a personal brand and about our corporate brands' ability to deliver under stressful circumstances. In this, buyers must measure the risk of moving to your brand and leaving a long-standing provider. Any supplier crossover bridge must be built strongly in order to make changes seem almost seamless. Believe me, this gives buyers sweaty palms, even if there are significant cost savings that we guarantee.

2)   **Buyers Make Almost No Mistakes**. This is a real "Pinocchio". I remember delivering a negotiation program to a sizable city hall group of executives, including the procurement department. This was a test to see which groups really needed negotiation training to help save the city money. The lead person from the procurement department attending said, "Negotiation training does not relate to me. I am a buyer." I asked what happens if you buy one million pieces of a product and it does not work as promised. She replied by saying, "Well, we would certainly never use that supplier again." This, my friends, is only the tip of the iceberg.

3)   **Buyers Are Financial Geniuses**. My flat comment is: "Not a chance." Buyers and sellers are equal in this measurement in my opinion. There is the one huge advantage that some buyers have had for some time over sellers, and it will continue to grow. It is database power. In the near future, it will be artificial intelligence. Here is a fact that should scare you. Over 50% of all stock trades now completed on all of the New York Stock Exchanges are executed by Quantitative Computer Systems looking for key words that trigger the buying and selling of $Billions of dollars of securities. Notwithstanding, I have deep respect for my buyer contemporaries and there are a few that really get my game on. Here are the people on the buying side that I have great respect for: Steve Cosic, Betty Roy, Donna

Welch, Gaye Mandel, and Greg Crombie. All of them managed bigtime media budgets. Steve Cosic was responsible for over $100 Million annually in media expenditures. Steve and Greg have since passed and I still miss them profoundly.

Nevertheless, as a seller, what advantages do buyers have that I should be really tuned into? Additionally, how do I try to prepare for, and hope to recognize, these buyer leverage points? I could give you a long list; instead, I will offer up three key advantages that buyers have over sellers. Buyers control their buying environment when sellers present proposals in buyer head offices. Buyers get paid to listen and observe body language. Buyers are risk agents and get paid to reduce seller margins. Therefore, they are adept at digging out deep seller value, which can be translated into savings. Let's unpack this a little more.

1)   **Buyers Control Their Environment**. I can remember walking into the media department of the Hudson's Bay Company and having their VP of media standing in the hallway just in front of us swinging a baseball bat hard enough to make a swoosh sound. He would follow that with, "So, what have you got for us today?" When I would walk into the Walmart head office, all the meeting rooms looked like faceless boxes with six chairs around a no-frills table and accompanied by a window in the meeting room door. The walls were bare. The room was booked in tight 30-minute in-tervals, so, at minute 25, someone would knock on the door indicating all within the meeting were on the clock. It felt like call control and pressure aimed at unnerving the sellers.

2)   **Buyers Are Expert Listeners & Body Language Specialists**. Some might say, "Pat, this is total cow pucky. How can you make such a bold statement?" I'm glad you asked. Buyers are forced to listen to detect seller weakness points. Buyers must boil down sellers' business cases in a few minutes and decide whether the discussion deserves an advance to a second meeting. I am going out on a limb here. I am going to claim that

buyers are more likely to be analytics and conciliation personality types who are better at listening and observing in a buyer's role. I will also claim that buyers are not great at presenting tough sales pitches and taking rejection in a seller's role.

3)   **Buyers Are Risk Agents**. Can you imagine, as a seller, sending out an RFBP to 100 of the top buyers in your business vertical for one million-dollar budgets only? What the heck is an RFBP? It is a Request for Buyer Proposal, of course. Also, included in your seller's 40-page RFBP would be specifications, pricing parameters, deadlines, and lots of small print that would make an eagle go crossed-eyed. Hmmmm, okay. How about a procurement-style cattle call of 40 buyers to appear at a seller's head office? The buyers will be there to present to a panel of sellers as to why these sellers should accept the buyers' measly $1 Million annual buyer budget. I can hear you thinking, "Pat you are out there." My wider point is that in a buyers' market the procurement situation is different. There are far too many sellers and not enough buyers. The buying side has an enormous advantage. Buyers can sift through well priced, competitive data at a pace that would make most sellers envious. Buyers control the game. They have a better handle on controlling time, risk, and what price they will accept.

Lessons Learned. Corporate sellers, I hope I have cleared up a few misconceptions about buyers. My advice to you is if you are going to sell in the buyer big leagues, you had better get some serious selling game on. The buyers are just as professional as you and they control most of the cards in the deck. Remember this and arrive prepared to play big ball.

You might be wondering how I can be so sure about all of the above examples. I am certain of them because I was a national Canadian print buyer for our newspaper company.

7

UNDERDOGS MAKE FEARLESS COMPETITORS

I have worked for so many underdog sales products that I can't remember all of the names of the media brands. My early "mud wrestling" days selling underdog products made me a fearless, cunning, and red-blooded seller. Some of you may cringe at the terms "cunning" and "red-blooded", but I can tell you that the passion in those descriptors cannot be faked.

Working for underdog, disruptive weekly and daily newspapers such as the *South Edmonton Times*, the *Oakville Journal Record*, and the *Calgary Sun* taught me how to be the hungriest dog on the street. I can tell you without hesitation that there are few stronger states of mind that beat hunger.

The cool thing about being an underdog seller is that if you can survive and pay your bills, there is really no big pressure on you. You can try all sorts of unusual ideas. To be candid, your sales manager hopes that "risk-on thinking" will be part of your sales profile. They want hungry sellers who bring ideas to customers that many top-dog corporate account managers are very reluctant to try.

As an underdog, I knew that I would not be receiving the lion share of any newspaper buyer's budget. This meant that I had to crank out more proposals, make more calls, and close more smaller deals than my uptown competitor. By selling to smaller customers, I was focused on selling flights of 6, 12, and 24 weeks of advertisements. Selling to one-time advertisers was a fiscal bust. The only exceptions were event-driven promotions such as Mother's Day, in which case you take what you can get from "orphan" advertisers.

While working at the *Oakville Journal Record* (OJR), a community newspaper, we had one of the coolest artists that one could ever hope to employ. His name is Steve Nease. Steve was not just our artist; he was our political cartoonist. As an artist, he combined the best of conventional art and cartooning line art. I love this hybrid. It fit perfectly with our advertising department because Steve's style was crisp, edgy, and whimsical. Steve's mind was wide open and still is today.

The Christmas selling season is critical in the newspaper business. The season starts right after back-to-school and is a horse race right through Boxing Day. It is outbound customer call madness. As I remember it, one of our cool local retailers was using a sketch of his store as a newspaper advertising logo. This was a neat concept. You see, Oakville was small enough that if you came to town and showed someone this logo, the locals could tell you where to find the store. It was small-town branding at its finest.

That particular fall, we were looking for a hook to drive last quarter sales. Our sales manager, Bill McConkey, envisioned a whole series of retail store fronts being turned into line art signatures. Steve Nease was invited to one of our weekly sales meetings. We circled around a pile of theme possibilities to drive multiple week advertising campaigns. Somehow, as a collective, we kept circling back to Bill's store front drawing idea. With Bill's encouragement, Steve agreed to create 21 replications of these store fronts. Once compiled, these drawings would be a collection of the most prominent stores in Oakville. The cool part was our competitors would not have access to these unique brand signatures. The sales team was pumped and intended to build these beauties into cash register-ringing, retail advertising campaigns. Talk about exciting. We had seven sales professionals on the retail team. Therefore, it meant each sales professional had three iconic drawings to sell in a campaign comprised of full pages right down to business card-sized advertisements. It was advertising planned with military precision because we wanted to surprise the market—and did we ever.

With Bill's vision and Steve burning the late-night oil, it happened. The OJR delivered ad campaigns and store front OJR newspaper sections that were very well received by our advertisers and their shoppers. This program grew much faster and much larger than we ever could have believed. This store front advertising format ran for years afterward and was submitted by the OJR for newspaper advertising creative awards. If you can believe it, after the OJR was purchased by our competitor, the store front sketch advertising model continued to grow and is still in demand to this day.

Lessons Learned. Selling in the underdog position can be a real catalyst for creative, passionate, and crafty deal-making. Executives who manage hungry underdogs know how to keep them lean and in the moment with tantalizing, hot opportunities. Underdogs understand that if someone hands them a great idea, they must examine it and not balk at it. Underdogs understand that no one is going to hand them a free dinner. Notwithstanding, first call, numeri uno, fat cat corporate sellers, beware. There is a hungry dog circling your bowl and it is fearless.

8

SELLING UP, ACROSS, AND AROUND

If you want to be very successful in the corporate sales world, you have to improve one essential skill. You have to learn to sell up, across, and around. By this, I mean that the corporate world has changed and become so idea-oriented that many groups of sales professionals actually have a say in who joins their sales group. In this case, it is about fit and potential collaboration opportunities for team members. In this vein and situation, you are selling across and around. Selling up is just as critical.

I believe that I have always been a multi-directional seller because I was always chasing after more knowledge in the various companies for which I worked. This meant I would contact senior managers across the country. I wanted to get their take and buy-in on subjects I believed were important to the growth and development of new products. I was not just making these calls to my senior advertising sales managers. I was talking to production, credit, and creative managers. I was selling wherever I needed help and information.

Don Fisher was my boss on the Southam retail team for many years. Don had been the president of a division of the Simmons Mattress Company. Don knew just about everything when it came to manufacturing, wholesale, retail, and customer research. He was one of the most enormously talented, humble, end-to-end business thinkers I have ever met. While my sales brothers and sisters were having lunch every day, I would tag Don and say, "Let's grab a 30-minute power walk around the block and stretch our legs. We will grab a quick sandwich on the return." Don knew right away what I was up to and he was always up for a walk and a chat. This gave me precious one-on-one time with him. It gave me time to test a huge lineup of ideas for which I had to get his blessing before implementing. If there were concerns, we would both work on a forward plan. To me, this was another kind of selling up in a low-stress manner.

Think about these power walks with Don this way. Would you rather be outdoors on a nice sunny day taking in a few rays while sales planning? Or, would you rather do the same planning in a stuffy, pressure-packed boardroom while staring at a clock? To me, it was a no-brainer. Today, I would call this communication, outdoor sales jamming.

There was one more huge advantage to selling up in my organizations. I got a reputation for being a positive risk-taker. Companies look for positive risk-takers because they know people with a risk profile such as mine are raring to try new ideas. Professionals with my profile test new approaches to selling and negotiation with whale-sized accounts.

Finally, when it came time to discuss quarterly budgets and year-end bonuses, those above me knew I always wanted to be part of the narrative, as opposed to taking what was offered. If I came back to them with a concern,

I had done my homework and was not backing down easily. I only had to learn this lesson once and it never happened again.

Lessons Learned. Please give thought to selling up, across, and around in your corporate world. Be bold. Be creative. Add some positive risk to your corporate sales world. Zoom-meet with whomever you can to improve the chances of your ideas moving up in the corporate food chain. Reach out and talk to as many smart people in your company as you can. Be brave and cross channels. Your senior managers will take note and engage you. Consider asking colleagues to join you outdoors at a picnic table for a meeting or a power walk. Remember, none of us is smarter than all of us.

9

ARE YOU A BUYER OR A SELLER?

As a young man, I worked in dangerous industrial settings. I have also worked in one of the most elite business settings in Canada during its glory days: the Toronto Star advertising department. Guess what? Both were unionized. The unions at the companies I worked for had mandates to be advocates for workers who could not speak for themselves.

When I worked at the International Harvester Company, just a couple of workstations away from where my Dad died 10 years earlier, I was approached by two union officials. I was told to slow down so that I did not ruin a job with a specific piece work time ticket. The job entailed smashing enormous cotter pins into a steel pipe with a hole drilled through it. Time ticket? My hands were numb after one shift.

When I worked at the Toronto Star as a sales representative, I was appointed union steward. Shortly after this appointment, I found myself in the middle of a company-wide strike. A wise-ass friend and colleague enrolled me in the strategy committee to shut the Toronto Star down during the strike. I was voted in as a strike captain. I ended up leading the creative department at the worst position at the Star: the back-loading dock. I cannot describe how far human civility can fall in a strike setting. In the last two instances, all of this happened when I was on the road, selling. I came back to the Star office and was shocked. The position imposed on me was a total eye-opener. Nevertheless, as I tell the rest of this story, you will know that I have experienced all the union exposure that one might hope to have in a lifetime. In my view, this Toronto Star strike should not have happened if everyone on both sides were listening, but this was not so.

Now, leap 15 years forward. It was approximately the year 2000. I walked up to the Starter at my local municipal golf course and asked if I could get a tee time as a single player. The starter looked out his shack window and said, "There is a threesome on the tee. Grab a ticket and I will slow them down. You are on the tee now." I rushed into the golf shop and there were 8 guys in front of me. I quickly explained my situation and offered to buy them all a beer if I could pay for my tee ticket and get out on the course. They listened and agreed. Beer is good.

After the 18 holes, I was waiting for the 8 gents at the club house and kept my promise with 8 frosty Canadian beers. May I repeat, "8 frosty Canadian beers" (Pause…meditation. Okay, I am back). Sitting with these gents, I asked them about their round of golf and what brought them to the club. As a local, I knew a lot of the players, but did not recognize them. One of them indicated that they were visiting Toronto to support the airplane mechanics at Air Canada. I asked them where they were from and what their role was. They said they were company managers and were visiting to help Canadians hold and grow $100,000 middle income class jobs.

I had been in business long enough to know that nobody identifies themselves as company managers, at least not in Canada. It is too vague. I asked them what union they were with and from what state in the United States. Their accents were mild, so I imagined them from the Midwest. I asked them what the potential strike issues were and how they were going to support the Canadians. I also asked them how they were going to solve the labour dispute. They just kept repeating their middle-income mantra when I queried them. Pausing, I tried a couple of different ways to ask the same question with no clearer answer.

There was a reflective beer-sipping moment. I asked them, "If you are helping with this negotiation, is your side the buyer or the seller?" This question totally blind-sided them, or, perhaps, they thought I was just another Canadian nut bar. They asked what buying and selling had to do with solving a labour negotiation.

I tried to explain my point by sharing that I was in sales and understood a bit about unions. I said, "In a customer negotiation, it is always understood that one side is selling value and the other side is digging for deeper value to buy at the best price." Nevertheless, I asked the U.S. union gents if they were customers or sellers in this negotiation. Were they buyers or sellers?

The union folk carefully walked me through their position. They believed that Air Canada was doing well and that asking for a list of needs from the union side was justified. They explained that any union action would be in kind with the Air Canada action. I shared that I believed all businesses need to be profitable and are always looking for efficiencies, even on the sales side. (Sometimes, sales groups change in size and shape.) I asked, "What new efficiencies is the union side bringing to the negotiation table, so that both sides can benefit?" I indicated that it might sound odd to them, but I believed that the union side was the selling side and the corporate side was the buying side in this particular case.

These eight gents were incredibly fair, honest, and civil in this discourse. They were quiet after I asked the above questions, but I did not press the gents. They were doing their job as they saw it. There was goodwill as we spoke. I think we all walked away with a new outlook on labour negotiation. I know I certainly learned.

I use the above Toronto Star and Air Canada examples because roles in a corporate sales negotiation can become entrenched. There are times when one or both sides do not understand that markets change and perceived value changes. Technology changes. Culture changes. Believe it or not, these dynamics can even happen in our own families when we negotiate with our loved ones.

Lessons Learned. Each negotiation is unique. Past negotiations can give us a sense of how problems were solved in that moment, but they do not always lay a predictable path in future negotiations. Conditions change. Negotiation teams change. Our approach to negotiation must always lie in the present, with an eye on the past and an ear to the future. Buyers and sellers can actually switch roles in a negotiation for periods of time. Always ask yourself, "As a corporate seller, am I a buyer or a seller at this moment?"

10

TOP 14 TRAITS OF CORPORATE SELLERS

The very best corporate sellers are specialized generalists. These best-of-breed sales professionals look at selling as a panoramic view. They see sales prospecting, consultative selling, and sales negotiation as one continuous conversation. Corporate sellers are the same as the rest of us in sales in that they are better at some things than others in their craft. I have noted over the years that corporate sellers do consistently exhibit 14 dominant traits. These traits mean corporate sellers are soon to arrive at their sales peak performance, and this optimal benchmark is an elite standard that sets them apart. They are gifted sales professionals, and their sales traits include the following.

1)   **Inquisitiveness**. By nature, people with inquisitive minds are able ask great open-ended questions. They think rapidly to the next level of open-ended questions before their customers have even answered the first

query. They are mental data miners. As a result, they quickly and concisely get to the root of their customer's needs, demands, and wants.

2)   **Strategy**. Strategic corporate sellers see customer engagements as a chessboard. They quickly assess the other side's strengths and weaknesses. They devise routes of cooperative engagement with plans and backup plans. Corporate sellers lull us to sleep. They comfort us, while they are gently closing routes of escape. They think strategically and act collaboratively.

3)   **Analytic process**. Here, we have the number-crunchers and the masters of logic. They induce outcomes and plans for deductive closure. Analytical thinkers bring out the beauty in numbers. They bring light to the shadows in chaos, which can confuse their customer partners in complicated long-term business dealings. Analytical corporate sellers think big and explain in simple terms.

4)   **Emotional intelligence**. Rather than IQ, it's EQ. It's a talent that helps you understand those around you without them saying much. Those corporate sellers with higher EQ detect body language, eye contact, changes in mood, and atmosphere. They sense the other side by reading the room. They have profound empathy.

5)   **Risk assessment**. This is really a combination of analytical thinking and emotional intelligence. It's how corporate sellers gain the most in a business deal, while inserting positive risk and still getting a deal done. When done masterfully, corporate sellers maintain a strong collaborative relationship with customer partners.

6)   **Mental agility**. This is truly a great gift, as it allows corporate sellers to change risk and tactical gears in a collaborative sales setting, and adapt to the other side without being detected. Mental agility makes us appear to be underwhelmed by quick changes in direction from our client

partner. It gives us the confidence to stay grounded in the present and get deals done that stand the test of time.

7)   **Time awareness**. Corporate sellers who have awareness of real time can pace a collaborative, corporate selling experience to their advantage. They know how to compress and decompress time. To a degree, it's like being a mental traffic cop.

8)   **Detail orientation**. Those corporate sellers who are detail-oriented know how to plan for a mission to get to closure rapidly. As an example, their cost modeling is so well-placed, they know precisely when to move to a close. Detail-driven corporate sellers also know that taking control of the wording in contracts has the potential to work to their advantage. Their advance reconnaissance reassures long-term customer partners.

9)   **Storytellers**. Raconteurs set the stage for corporate customer engagements with their ability to weave opposing interests together. They know how to prime the pump. They add in anecdotal references to help customer partners understand why certain measures are recommended. Storytellers make us feel good and help both sides cross the finish line to a positive deal. Storytellers really understand how to get our emotional brain in a nice, fun place. Super storytellers help corporate customers remember their stories, and this is where the sharing begins. This melding of the minds is a huge step toward building trust. Please read my other two books, *Unlocking Yes, the Revised Edition* or *Perpetual Hunger*, because I dedicate an entire lesson on my storytelling model. Once you understand the model, you can build your own. I cannot tell you how important this is to living your sales dreams.

10)   **Killer instinct**. Those with a killer instinct are not afraid to seize an opportunity with a corporate customer partner that may not appear again. Corporate sellers know some moments of truth that involve creativity to close deals need an extra little push. This instinct is also about knowing

when the other side is ready, but needs to be reassured. Corporate sellers with a killer instinct know perseverance is just part of the collaborative deal-closing process.

11)   **Hunger**. Living in a perpetual state of hunger is a way of thinking that not everyone possesses. Some of us are hungry for the great satisfaction of closing a piece of business. Others have short bursts of hunger in closing out on new business. We become satisfied and pull back. The very best corporate sellers are so hungry for new business that this thought process fills their minds until it is time to stop, and not before.

12)   **Discipline**. Corporate sellers with great discipline know how to plan for a mission to close a sale with great customer partners as quickly as is needed. Disciplined corporate sellers always have a game plan. Their sales scripting and cost modeling are so well placed that they know exactly when to close. They warm their customer partners with their advance reconnaissance. They soothe with probing trial closes to uncover the moment of opportunity to get a collaborative "Yes."

13)   **Creativity**. As a corporate seller, creativity can reveal itself in several ways. While I was in the media business, our visual products provided a great gateway for corporate sellers in our vertical to be creative. For corporate sellers, there is also an opportunity to grow the customer's business and our own using creative, eye-popping incentive proposals. These proposals offer exceptional value to the customer, while growing our year-over-year budgets with the customer in tandem. We all grow revenue by exploring creativity in incentive plans.

14)   **Patience**. They say that patience is a virtue. I think in life and in corporate sales, patience is something bigger. Patience is a test of our ability to adapt to situations where all of our sales cards have been played. Nothing more can be added to the stew. The sales dinner is complete. As corporate sellers, we are just waiting for our corporate sales guest to sit at the table

and enjoy our deep-value sales feast. Where big money is concerned, you cannot force anything. Large corporate deals that are forced will be filled with regret and worse.

Lessons Learned. So, here's a question to all corporate sales managers out there. "How does your sales team measure up with the above traits? Understanding this, how are you going to improve their skill traits?" With Centroid Sales and Negotiation Training, the above skills can be learned or improved exponentially.

11

OWN THE ROOM

In the late 1990s, someone got an idea that the FSI (Free Standing Insert) business needed to be placed under a microscope to illuminate any bad practices that might be taking place in the industry in Canada. Insert delivery companies here were operating with amazing efficacy, considering the size and complexity of geography in those days. You see, Canada is a long ribbon of population density along the U.S. border with one or two anomalies, such as the city of Edmonton in the north of Alberta.

Canadian cities are made up of large clusters of people who live in four-season dwellings, similar to what you would find in Chicago. We have homes and apartment buildings. We have farms and country properties similar to the United States. The biggest problem that the insert delivery business faces is gaining entry to closed-access apartments and delivering to dwellings way out in the country in a cost-efficient manner.

Notwithstanding, the retail industry, whose inserts/flyers are delivered primarily by newspapers, decided they needed an association. In a blink, the Flyer Distributions Standards Association (FDSA) was born. With the birth of any association comes several committees and lots of deep thinking. The deep thinkers are led by very deep thinkers called "Chairs". I was a Founding Director of the FDSA, owing to my flyer responsibilities with the Hollinger Newspaper Group (Canada's largest newspaper company). I did not want to be a chairperson and rather enjoyed sitting on various committees where I preferred to report my observations back to Hollinger's 125+ newspapers.

The Chair of the National Dwelling Count Committee (yes, that was a real committee) was released from her job shortly before one of our annual meetings. With the annual meeting of the FDSA came a series of presentations on the progress of each committee. Typically, these presentations were 10 to 15 minutes long. Sitting at these meetings were the senior representatives of most of Canada's major retailers, newspapers, and flyer delivery companies. Also present were several of my company VPs and SVPs. I was the lucky soul who was chosen to replace the Dwelling Chair at the podium, presenting to about 125–150 business executives in a theatre setting.

The night before the annual meeting, the two organizers of the meeting emailed me a six-page report of the dwelling count portfolio. There were tons of details in this presentation. Knowing this, I prepared. The day of the meeting, there was a lot of hustle and bustle around the podium just before the meeting got underway. I walked up to the organizers to inquire how things were going. All I remember hearing was, "Pat, there was a change in planning late last night and your dwelling report has been reduced to three slides." I stared at these three slides and thought, how do I manage this? I am going to be presenting momentarily, after the opening remarks have been made by the leadership team. I can't even read these slides fast enough to create a new flow in my mind. My preparation was based on six slides. Suddenly, I am introduced to the audience and the place falls into silence.

I strolled up to the podium. I turned around and looked for one key word on the jumbo screen. I started to speak in a firm voice with my hand directed at the slide. I started talking about the key word in its context. Next, I moved out from behind the podium. I walked up to the audience and gave a 10-minute talk on the progress that I believed the dwelling committee had made in the past year. I did not look at my new slides—not even once. Ten minutes of public speaking is a long time. That said, if you pace evenly, punctuate, and act energized, who the heck in the audience, including my boss, was going to know the difference? You know who? Nobody.

When I went back to college for the third time to complete a program in Management Studies, I was taking four courses simultaneously. I attended classes at night and on the weekends while working full-time. To accomplish this, I developed a study ritual that allowed me to digest massive amounts of information for short periods of time, and later regurgitate this data for exams. As I entered university in my late 20s, I perfected this study method and wrote some amazing exams. For this particular FDSA audience, I decided to overprepare. I had a talking point from each of the six pages drilled into my mind. All I needed was a key word to start my presentation.

Lessons Learned. Trust your instincts, stay in the present, and block out the noise. Be your own best friend. Prepare professionally, drink in the moment, and smile bigtime. Own the room.

12

DON'T DO IT

While working for a national entertainment magazine, I was on a sales tear that many of us dream about. Initially, I was hired to call on the national advertising agencies in Toronto and I had some great success. I tagged along with the advertising director who was working on a plan to offer General Motors a deal it could not refuse. It was a diamond-level sponsorship of the Winter Olympic Games, which we had big plans to cover. It was a truly exciting time to be selling into the national automotive category. In truth, I needed a rest from my days in retail sales for the company. The problem for me was that the magazine desperately needed new revenue. It was totally apparent to me that the current magazine sales team did not know how to call on big retailers.

Before I knew it, the advertising director was inviting me to lunch to do strategy planning to capture new retail accounts. I shared a few opportunity ideas that I observed the magazine was missing. Before long, I was selling to clients that were new to the magazine. Entertainment magazines match up naturally with a lot of retail categories. For instance, I sold a paint and wallpaper retailer into our magazine that had never considered us before and it worked very well. Anything related to entertainment, home fashion, food, alcohol, automotive, automotive services, gardening, home improvement, and restaurants all worked in an entertainment content environment. Even elements of fashion worked in an entertainment category, but not every category worked.

Entertainment magazines, like a lot of other print products, were under pressure from all kinds of new media competitors. One of our major advertisers at the time was Sears. Shortly after our retail strategic planning sessions, the advertising director invited me to look at the magazine's revenue reports. He wanted my thoughts on the magazine's current status. I said, "You are in trouble if you expect Sears to continue at this expenditure pace." I have paraphrased this because my response was a little more jocular, and this was well before anyone really new how bad it was at Sears. Obviously, this was not at all what the advertising director wanted to hear, much less from me. Nonetheless, I told him I could find him new money, and I did. He was under immense pressure from the publisher of the magazine, and so much so that he and the company parted company shortly after.

Prior to the next advertising director being hired, our Publisher, who was short on patience, called the whole sales and promotion team to a meeting. She said, "All of our jobs are on the line if we do not turn this magazine around shortly." A sales colleague we will call "A" looked over at me after her comment. He had the expression of a man "chewing on an angry wasp." After this firecracker sales meeting, our promotions manager disappeared into his office and made a few phone calls. He soon announced he had taken a job with another company and departed just like that. This made the atmosphere at the magazine even tenser. When people start pulling up stakes over the content of a meeting, you know the sales culture is getting a little crispy.

Within a few short weeks, the magazine was introduced to our new Advertising Director. He had both a newspaper and magazine background. He also knew he was replacing a person who just left the company in haste. Our new Director was under the microscope to produce results for our Publisher. He had to make it happen no matter what, and he did so in the time we worked together. Revenue grew and the retail category grew. We were pulling in a lot of new advertisers, including a department store promoting its "Discount Fashion Department". (Read more on this crusher deal in *Unlocking Yes, the Revised Edition.*)

My sales run continued and I grew my retail sales territory by a whopping 25% the next year. My new boss largely left me to close business as I saw it using crafty and creative sales proposals. I would drag my Director out on calls when I needed some extra muscle. Occasionally, he would hit me with a new retail product category to chase. We both understood what the edge of our magazine's sales results efficacy was for advertisers. On one particular day, he called me in and said, "I want you to call on Business Depot and get a deal done." The VP of Marketing at Business Depot was a golf buddy and long-time friend of mine. Given my relationship with my friend at Business Depot, you would probably believe this call and sale was an "open net goal", as we say here in Canada. Not so. The SMB (small, medium business category), which Business Depot served, was not in our wheelhouse from a reader's perspective. I resisted my Director's request at first citing our reader profile. To me, this call request was a total stretch. Regardless, I knew that eventually it would be a demand from my boss, so I set up the meeting with Business Depot.

I developed a test program proposal for the meeting, but as I was driving to the call, my gut went off. I have a long-standing business belief: "friends first...business second". Nevertheless, if my belief was real, how could I make this call? In making this call, I satisfied my boss, but I could not sell the wrong product to the wrong customer, let alone a close friend. The more I thought about my dilemma, the more it ate at me. My inner compass took over during the call and my face told the whole story. If you are good at reading body language, I looked like a guy who was placed in an "axe fight" with grim orders to come in second. I am sure my friend at Business Depot picked me off. He was kind enough to let me finish the pitch, knowing I did not want him to buy. He read me perfectly.

If you are a sales manager reading this right now, you might be saying, "Hey, Mr. Compassionate, you just blew that call." You know, you'd be justified to think this way. On the other hand, I didn't want a bad recommendation to ruin a relationship that could later be tapped if our magazine suddenly shifted its content toward home business. If we decided to build a small business section in our magazine, Business Depot would be my first call. I'd have been all over it like a big kid on a bag of candy.

Lessons Learned. Regardless of massive pressure to perform, stop. Stand sure. Think about the customer first. Misguided proposals must be treated as such. Great customers deserve nothing but our very best "value-delivering ideas." Most in sales have a true north. If closing a sale with the wrong customer is ever in doubt, listen to your gut. Listen to your true north. Don't do it regardless of the pressure from senior management. As corporate sales professionals, our personal brand is our equity. If you have no equity, you are disposable. If you have no equity, you may even be a deficit. Finally, think about your family and your business legacy. How do you want to be remembered when all is said and done?

13

IMPORTANCE OF MOMENTUM IN ACCOUNT CONVERSION

The daily newspaper business is an anomaly in today's Internet content ocean. Newspapers check facts.

When I was National Insert Distribution Manager for the largest newspaper company in Canada, we had a challenge in some of our markets. Competitors to our daily newspapers had cut costs to the bone and were taking market share of large insert accounts and bolting them down.

In one western market in particular, Kamloops, our brand the *Kamloops Daily News* had lost most of its insert business to a feisty, weekly newspaper. I was approached by the Advertising Manager at the *Kamloops Daily* for some help.

The Advertising Manager from the *Kamloops Daily* was convinced he had the same distribution depth as his competitor, but he could not absolutely prove it. It was total delivery numbers against total delivery numbers. This called for a fact check.

At the time, I was working on a fact-checking process for our daily newspapers across Canada, which I referred to as a "reconciliation". I was on a mission to reconcile each of our markets to understand our verifiable delivery penetration of homes, apartments, and rural areas. The thinking was that if we actually counted where we could and could not deliver, we had a point of difference with this knowledge. The next step was to perform the same reconciliation exercise on our competitors' distribution numbers. The intent was to challenge our competitors' insert distribution figures. We also intended to increase our verification processes to enhance this new approach to market penetration reconciliation. Next, we matched this information on closed apartment building access and known dwelling vacancy rates within these buildings.

We had one other critical advantage. Being a daily newspaper meant that our customers were buying their newspapers and wanted them delivered to their homes, apartments, or condos. The household delivery was a snap. Our delivery personnel just dropped the newspaper off at the householder's front door. The apartments and condos were a trickier story because the vast majority of these buildings were closed access. This meant that our newspaper carriers had to arrive at an agreement with the apartment building owners. We signed these agreements to gain access to a front door key so our newspaper carriers could deliver to the unit doors of our readers. Our weekly newspaper delivery competitors could not secure these premium front door key arrangements with the apartment building management teams. We were onto something big.

You might be thinking, why does all this research matter to advertisers who print and deliver inserts? It all has to do with the cost containment of printing and delivery. This included not disturbing to customers who did not want flyers. It also had to do with wasted flyers that would ultimately be trashed if they were delivered to customers who did not find them appealing. Our research ultimately led to savings for our insert customers. This gave us a point of difference and leverage.

I laid out the above city householder reconciliation program to the *Kamloops Daily* Advertising Manager and asked him if he could match all of these quality points. Next, I asked him how many advertiser incentive plans he could think up. I asked him to double-check with other successful newspapers to understand their customer enhancements to the actual insert delivery. This Advertising Manager was hungry and did absolutely everything I recommended and more. It was a total transformation of how the *Kamloops Daily News* communicated with huge insert customers, some of whom delivered flyers 52 weeks a year or more.

The reason this was so transformational was the *Kamloops Daily News* re-established itself as a brand leader. The *Daily News* new value proposition was not based on price. Its value proposition was now based on quality delivery and quality household research, building a new found sense of confidence. Confidence is a game changer. You cannot buy or make confidence up. You have to grow and own the feelings of confidence, organically. It is bigger than a feeling. It is a glow that only comes from believing your brand is so superior to the market standard that you are bulletproof in front of customers. This kind of confident attitude is a market momentum game changer.

With this new found mojo, a lot of client presentation momentum started to work its way into the narrative. Now, the *Daily News* was combining great proposals with support from local retail store managers to win flyer customers back. In the beginning, it was small to medium-sized retail flyer customers. Our delivery service not only lived up to its new brand promises, it was also reshaping the on-page newspaper advertisements these smaller advertisers were placing. As a rule, when the insert business moves, so do the run of press (ROP) advertisements. This was a double-whammy win for the *Kamloops Daily News*.

After many months, and many calls with wonderful proposals, the customer conversion to the *Kamloops Daily News* started to close in on a 50% market share. This kind of shift in momentum is what makes the biggest national flyer advertisers take notice. The shift in momentum was so remarkable that cold calls to large advertisers became informed calls. A few more wins later and the *Kamloops Daily News* had completed a tipping point. Almost every advertiser opened its doors to great conversations, accompanied by calls from the local store managers. Now, the local store managers were further driving momentum by enquiring about changing from our competitor to the *Kamloops Daily News* delivery system.

I am certain that this change in momentum for the *Daily News* in the Kamloops marketplace was determined by a passion to change and win. This momentum shift was not a landslide, but rather a slow, planned, and deliberate march forward. All of the efforts between our corporate sales offices, the *Kamloops Daily News*, and all local stakeholders were simpatico. Momentum is a sales game changer and absolutely vital to large account conversions. The neat part of what I have shared with you is that this kind of momentum shift is repeatable and necessary. If any business wants to become a market leader, it has to plan to make changes and march forward, driving momentum.

Lessons Learned. Never underestimate a smaller competitor; they are often agile and opportunistic. The facts matter and must be verified and reconciled. When weak, own the narrative and seek out cutting-edge solutions. Changing processes takes time and requires commitment. Momentum is transformational and builds confidence; it especially matters when big customer budgets are in play.

Here is a question for sales managers out there who are struggling to win back market share: "Are you ready to commit to shifting the momentum in order to grow in your market vertical?"

14

PRESSURE

One of the things that separates major corporate account management from local account management is pressure. I am sure the drums are starting to beat after local account managers read this statement. Notwithstanding, the argument I am presenting here is true. I have lived both sales roles as a local account manager and a major corporate account manager, so I can attest to this argument from a boots-on-the-ground perspective.

Nevertheless, the question is "Why?" Let me explain. When a major account manager is working on a multi-million-dollar deal with a long-standing customer and the customer does not get her/his way at the negotiation table, the heat starts to ratchet up. Internal reports are written by the account manager, and senior management starts to take notice. This creates more heat.

Another layer to this conversation is how the local stakeholders of the corporate company feel about impending deals with a major customer. If prices are reduced owing to a need to stay competitive, both corporate and local markets must adjust their costs and spending budgets. This creates even more heat.

If the deal with a large customer dies and millions of dollars are in play, job losses are the next layers of heat. From my perspective, this is the most damning and pressure-packed situation of all.

As I have mentioned in both of my sales books, *Unlocking Yes, the Revised Edition* and *Perpetual Hunger*, a large deal for me back in the mid-1990s was approximately $13 Million with a single account. There was no committee of signatures on the contract; it was just the customer's signature and mine. The value of money doubles about every 7–10 years. Now, think about the pressure in today's dollars and you get a sense of how many middle-income jobs were at stake if I lost a deal of this magnitude. I am being conservative when I say that well over 100 jobs were in play. This is big-time heat.

If you have never felt the cold sweat rolling down your back in the middle of a $13 Million deal coming to closure, I can tell you that the pressure is almost indescribable. Days, weeks, and even months of preparation may be required to close a single deal. It is no fun waking up several times a night to leave yourself voicemail messages because you are too tired to make notes that would not be readable in the morning.

Once the deal is signed and on the books, a post-mortem is completed on the pros and cons of the deal. Preparation for next year's contract negotiation starts all over again. This is why major account management makes young men and women grey early. It's all about the pressure.

Patrick Tinney

In *Unlocking Yes, the Revised Edition*, I have written strong lessons on how to handle heavy pressure. One tip to reduce pressure involves your jaw. Drop your jaw an inch and the stress in your face will reduce. You can drop your jaw without even opening your mouth. This technique has worked for me when I needed to take all of the stress out of my face. This jaw-drop technique gives you a sense of peace. Try it now. It works, doesn't it?

Lessons Learned. Pressure, stress, and heat are all a part of corporate big money sales. The trick is to manage it. When you head into important customer meetings and negotiations, be the most prepared person in the room. Rest well and eat well. Focus on the present and win. Pressure and stress can be managed.

PART II – EXPLORATION

15

CORPORATE CALL OBJECTIVES

Let's begin by stating that "All call objectives for accounts from large and small businesses really matter." It is just foolhardy to drop in on a customer without a call objective. Unless the customer is one of your best friends, you are going to eat into their time and tick them off.

Now, let's jump into a large corporate account setting. You would think that everyone who calls on corporate accounts have the above figured out and would not go there. Wrong. I have groaned through dozens of what I would call useless, boring, condescending, and bogus large account corporate customer meetings with company corporate stakeholders. These same company stakeholders should have been more adult.

Here are 12 must-call planning tips. I trust these tips will help you to be the sizzle that customers want to see.

1)   Many corporate buyers I called on worked insanely long hours for pay that just did not justify their great professional efforts. Therefore, please make a point of presenting new research, new product ideas, and competitive analysis that will give your buyer a competitive advantage. A customer that is given a competitive advantage will love you for this gift. Help your buyer be seen as the smartest buyer in their company.

2)   Since corporate buying departments are suffering cutbacks with the rest of the marketplace, buyers love new creative ideas. The reason is that every part of their company is so stretched that they can no longer afford to buy these ideas, unless they are facing emergencies. Buyers must rely on suppliers to fill this void.

3)   Plan your calls when your customers are at their brightest and most rested. This is different for every customer, so make a point of asking when they are most open to calls that are critical to their business.

4)   If yours is an emergency call with the customer, find out when they will take these types of calls. I worked with a Walmart buyer who started work at 5 a.m. He hated to drive in Toronto's insane morning traffic. For emergencies, 7 a.m. calls with this buyer were accepted.

5)   If your sales manager is accompanying you on a sales call, make sure she/he is up to date on your client's critical issues. Please make sure your manager understands his/her role in the meeting. Craft and rank your customer questions by dollar value. Make sure one of you is the note-taker. Listen to answers with great focus. If a customer gives you a piece of insider information, capture it in detail. Do a call post-mortem while your minds are fresh. This is critical.

6)   If you have an out-of-town regional manager who wants to meet with your corporate account, please make sure the meeting is not a grip and grin with a swag bag full of shiny junk. Nothing ticks corporate customers

off more. Remember, there are corporate policies that govern gifts of any kind to some buyers. If out-of-towners want meetings, make sure they are packing serious, local intelligence.

7)   If your call is over a lunch, please understand point #6. Your customers may be forced by corporate policy to buy their own lunch. Think this through. Be smart, and do not take them to a $100-a-plate restaurant. These same buyer companies probably have a lunch co-pay limit.

8)   Lunch these days is an hour, not two or three hours, with corporate customers. Respect this. With new artificial intelligence monitoring, the buyer's company will measure how long they are at lunch. Don't put your customer at risk by not planning well.

9)   Be sure each call you make with your customer has a product update, with an information gathering component. Make sure this call has an advance or a close element to it. We are not in the continuation business anymore.

10)   Customers love competitive information on their largest rivals. Any dish you can provide them will help your buyer shine in front of his/her superiors.

11)   Treat your corporate buyers as trusted friends or even family. All of our roles in both sales and procurement are tough these days. To a degree, we are all in this buying and selling tornado together, and we must all prosper by covering each other's best interests.

12)   Think about your long-term personal brand with your important corporate customers. This mindset will determine how much trust they will place in you. Earn trust by displaying your professionalism in every call you make with them.

Lessons Learned. Be a demand seller. Think like an insider and sizzle. Your customers will love you for it. Just think, this is all based on simply planning your call objectives. Finally, every call you make to an important customer must be of value to them and presented in a low self- interest manner.

16

WHY CUSTOMER CORPORATE CULTURE MATTERS

When you are heading into an important corporate sales negotiation, it is to your advantage to take special notice of your customer's corporate culture. Why, you ask? The answer is embedded in the values expressed within the walls of your customer's offices.

If all you did was take note of how your important customer's furnishings are arranged in their buyer waiting area and, ultimately, their buyer meeting rooms, you are actually learning about how they think. You are learning about what they value.

When I used to call on Walmart head office in Canada, it was very clear that their buyer waiting and meeting rooms dripped with formality and austerity. Their buyer waiting room was designed to alert buyers that they were about to engage in a different buyer experience with Walmart. For example, all of the chairs on which the sellers would be seated waiting for buyer meetings pointed in one direction like you see in a classroom. If you wanted to buy a soda pop in the waiting room, the price was almost at cost. Everything was bare bones.

When you moved into Walmart's meeting rooms, they were booked in tight 30-minute intervals. There were no pictures on the walls. The rooms were small, only accommodating about six people. The furniture was Spartan. All of these cultural clues are designed to send buyers messages such as:

1) Get to the point.

2) We mean business.

3) Your time is limited.

4) If we think lean, what should you be thinking?

This is only one corporate buying illustration. The wider point is that if you understand your customer's corporate culture, you are actually trying to think like they do. You are being observant and empathetic. You are trying to understand their psyche and patterns for doing business. You are learning what standards they expect so they will feel comfortable with you. They know that you de-risk their buying decisions. Remember, after you finish negotiating with your buyers, they have to take your proposal and sell it internally to their management team. These brave buyers represent you and your proposals in front of their stakeholders at their own peril. This is their understanding of risk management.

To be really successful with important customer culture, it is wise to try and mirror their value system. Try to speak using the language and terms they use so you sound more like an insider. We, as businesspeople, like to do business with people who think and speak as we do.

By blending into your customer's corporate culture, you become someone who they feel comfortable sharing ideas with. This gets us to the trusted level of a collaborative partner. If we bring ideas to our customers in a low self-interest, trusted partner manner, there is a greater chance they will believe in our true intent in sales and negotiations.

There is yet another level to understanding your customer's culture, and that is to do with understanding their forward planning and aspirations. This means that you are actually trying to think like their senior management team. When you are thinking in an aspirational manner through your customer lens, you really do have an amazing opportunity. It is an opportunity to help them grow their business, and by your actions, grow your own business in tandem.

Lastly, one of the keys to understanding your customer's corporate culture is to clearly understand their corporate social and environmental sustainability efforts. Often, this type of information is available on their website along with one more important piece of information: their cherished charities. Corporate culture is often watermarked with great social and philanthropic efforts to make communities and even the world a better place.

Lessons Learned. My greatest advice to all sellers is to do your homework on your customer's corporate culture. Please work to understand their deepest promises, aspirations, and opportunities. Put all of this information together and you are no longer just a sales professional selling stuff; you become one of them. In a customer relationship, you want to be a trusted sales partner that everyone wants to greet, listen to and share ideas with, and, ultimately, close deals that stand the test of time. Note to self: corporate culture matters in corporate sales.

17

SOMEBODY IS WATCHING YOU

For the most part, customers are pleasant when they greet you as a sales professional at their place of business. Both parties are on time for the meeting and the meeting closes on time with both parties having some follow-up work to do, if a great idea is to move forward. This is normal. If the client is late for a meeting, there is always a quick explanation and a terse apology. Everyone just gets on with the meeting. Both parties go about clocking their meeting objectives. Sometimes, you get the client who is always late. They expect sales professionals to be on time for the meeting, just in case the buyer is actually on time once a year. They rarely apologize for being obscenely late and expect the seller to suck up the lost selling time. This is the life of a sales professional dealing with buyers of all shapes and sizes.

As a seller, I had a trait that I was born with. For some reason, I have an internal clock that tells me what time of the day it is and even drives me to be early for most appointments I have booked for the day. I was this way before computers and cell phones. My clients loved this because they knew I would be there on time, or I would send a message advising the client of my estimated time of arrival. For important meetings, I was always about 30 minutes early so I could peacefully digest the content of my client meeting. This left me precious time to focus on the client during our meeting, to truly hone in on their concerns and how I would address them. To me, this is normal. I even went through a period when I worked at the Toronto Star (Canada's largest daily newspaper) where I refused to wear a watch. I did this because my sales director could care less what my sales numbers were, and I was crushing my numbers. Guess what? Even without a watch, I never missed or botched an appointment. This drove my immediate boss crazy, and he told me so, face to face with his veins popping out of his neck.

Fast forward a decade. I was now a Retail Manager with one of the magazine divisions of Hollinger/CanWest newspapers after a prosperous stint as the number one retail sales representative in our corporate head office. My largest customer, the Hudson's Bay Company (HBC), insisted that I be included on customer golf outings, even though I was no longer serving them. These golf events were always held on Saturday's at the best golf clubs we could secure tee times with around Toronto.

The Retail Manager on the newspaper side was old school. He worked 9 to 5 on the button. Rather than joining his sales reps for lunch, he would lock his windowed glass office and put his feet up on his desk. At lunch, he read a newspaper and ate take-out. It was a ritual and I could see a disaster looming. This type of physical behaviour is contagious in sales organizations and must be weeded out quickly.

Now, let's go back to our golf outing. My former Director of Procurement at HBC, Steve Cosic, and I were about to tee off on the first tee box. Our newspaper Retail Sales Manager was not to be seen or heard from. He didn't even call us on his cell. I asked Steve if he wanted to tee off or wait, and he said, "Let's go, Pat." His comment had no emotion in it. On the second hole, still no Retail Sales Manager. Steve leaned over to me and said, "I doubt he will show up at all and this is not the first time, it is all the time." I was shocked to say the least. On the fifth hole, the Retail Sales Manager suddenly roared on to the golf course, blaming his girlfriend for moving his golf clubs into her car. He complained that he did not have access to her keys even though they lived together. It was an ugly, uncomfortable day. This sales manager was removed from his duties shortly after. Thank God.

There is a funny thing about time. Nobody owns it. Everybody owns it. Everyone claims it. Some could care less about it. One thing I am absolutely sure of is that somebody is watching you and it is likely your customer. Customers watch how you use time. Customers do this because they know if they place their trust in you, eventually something will go wrong in business. It always does. The customer, who places their trust in how you use time, knows that when something goes off the rails with their business, you will be the first on the scene. You will be organizing the chaos and getting the customer's business back up on its feet, running full tilt as usual. Remember, somebody is watching you.

Lessons Learned. What if you were the customer? What kind of customer would you be? Would you respect your sales professional's time? I ask these questions because I became a print buyer for the company. Guess what? I ran crisp, lean meetings with my suppliers. Add it up.

18

BRAND ALIGNMENT REALLY MATTERS

Brand alignment in the contemporary sense is the alignment of all communication, cultural, and marketing efforts. This presents a brand as one continuous stream of thought to the consumer.

Alternatively, we want to present brand alignment as an alignment of corporate position in the market, relative to our clients and our selling peers. In a corporate sales negotiation, brand alignment has the potential to greatly influence our plans and backup plans.

Brand alignment for corporate partners could mean that we have customers, standards of excellence, or aspirations in common. These common elements naturally create an attraction for doing business together. Therefore, negotiating with a business partner whose needs profile fits our own makes for a matching or more leveled playing field. For example, in a previous life, I worked in the daily newspaper business. The closest match we had from a customer market profile perspective was major department stores. Research at the time pointed out that our daily newspaper readers were also very much aligned to the major department store customer ideal. This did not mean our business negotiations were "open net goals." It only meant that we both understood we had a lot of common ground that was compelling.

This alignment can happen anywhere in the business spectrum, from the ultra-high end of the business market to the low end of the business market. The cliché, "Birds of a feather flock together" comes to mind.

Nevertheless, if direct brand alignment is a benefit to both parties in a business negotiation, what does it mean for businesses that are interested in each other, but are further up or down the ideal pecking order? In a word, it's a "challenge."

In Toronto, we are blessed with four daily newspapers. To one degree or another, all of these newspapers are very well aligned to specific readers and advertisers. This means that they are in a ranked pecking order, up or down. In this setting, residing in the first or second market preference position with an advertiser is a much sought-after negotiation position. Residing in the third or fourth market preference positions becomes a negotiation challenge. Those daily newspapers on the perimeter high or low market positions have a huge challenge convincing advertisers that they are simpatico with opposite brand customers and quality requirements.

We have used daily newspapers as an example, but the same conversation about brand alignment in business could just as easily been shifted to home appliances, smart phones, fashion, or packaged goods.

Elements that equalize a lack of brand alignment at the bargaining table include creativity, innovation, quality, technology, timing, and price.

Creativity: Customers buy creative ideas over stuff any day of the week. Our company may be in the number three pecking position, but if we have creative solutions for a customer that attract new markets and add value, this is a great brand alignment equalizer.

Innovation: This is where we take unique brand parts and do something really neat to help our customer be smarter, faster, or better. If we can show a customer how to make money, we are bound to get a longer client engagement. Innovation is an equalizer.

Quality: Having access to different iterations of our product in various sizes, styles, positions, formats, or colour is an attention-grabber. If our company has the ability and agility to modify quality of a product to suit a budget or a marketplace, we are showing great flexibility. Guess what? We have another brand alignment equalizer.

Technology: Lots of customers love to be on the cutting edge of technology to give them an advantage in the market over their competitors. Technology may be something our company owns and has already paid for. It could be a new use of the Internet. It could be as simple as a new use for a symbol. Just think, a few years ago, hardly anyone had heard of a "Quick Response Code." For those who first adopted QR codes, they had a period of stylish, nerdy uniqueness so sought after in today's fickle consumer and business market.

Timing: Finding or saving time has the potential to give customers a strategic advantage over competitors and, quite possibly, save them money in the process. This is another great brand alignment equalizer.

Price: We have purposely saved price until last because anyone can lower price without thinking about the long-term ramifications this causes their brand and the very alignment they are seeking with a potentially important customer.

Lessons Learned. If we are lowering price for a well-placed strategy—bravo! If we are lowering price to maintain market share and keep feeding the troops, that's brave, but what is our exit plan? If we are buying business to make it to the next round of payments, I say, "Over to you."

When our company is trying to solve the problem of brand alignment in corporate sales and negotiation, we make sure our team does a customer needs assessment first. Think creativity, innovation, quality, technology, and timing to level the playing field. Leave price for last.

19

MEANINGFUL RESEARCH MOVES CORPORATE CUSTOMERS

Research really does interest corporate customers. This is exactly why large sellers of products and services spend so much money buying research, contributing to, research and creating their own in-house research.

Before database and global positioning systems (GPS) were available, I was interested in mapping research. I was fascinated by basic demographics and the positioning of my large retail corporate clients' store locations in major cities in Canada. I knew large retailers were always on the lookout for pockets of customers that matched their ideal customer profiles.

In the case of major department stores, their ideal customer was: 1) Female, 2) Mid-to-Better Income, and 3) Families with Children. When you group these three demographic areas together, you get accumulators. Accumulators are family groups who buy personal fashion and home fashion for all within their orbit. As an account manager who called on all retail sectors and the advertising agencies they employed, I used to watch this data like a hawk. I was always on the lookout for ways to bring greater value to my whale-sized accounts.

As I started to play with maps as a research tool, it was more a way to gain some wall space in my media buying customers' offices. For instance, I had my art department build 14" × 20" maps of major cities in Canada with the Hudson's Bay department store locations depicted with dots by postal area. In Canada, we call these postal geographic pockets FSAs or Forward Sortation Areas. In the United States, similar geographic units are called Zip Codes. To finish these maps, I would frame them with the Hudson's Bay company logo right next to our daily newspaper logo. It was a way to illustrate partnership and dominance for both of our companies and brands in each major market. My management team loved it when they walked into a Hudson's Bay office and saw our company with such presence in these corporate offices. I am sure my competitors just cringed when they saw the maps.

Shortly after developing this initial set of maps for my department store customers, I made a career move. I moved to our entertainment magazine that provided blanket circulation in all the cities it was offered. I wanted to sell major retail accounts into the magazine, but I needed a catalyst. Then it hit me. I needed to show large Drug, Food, and Junior and Major Department Store locations via maps. It would illustrate our entertainment magazine penetration by a major market with an overlay of the above retail store locations. It was a huge story to share. There was one more element that tipped the scales in my favour. Most of the above stores were starting to sell into each other's product categories, primarily to get at female and family shoppers. Through the mapping process stacking all drug, food, and department stores on top of each other, I could show the intense competitive sets for the same customers by market.

I approached my management team at the magazine and got a green light for the budget to produce the maps. This project was big because the number of store locations was eye popping across Canada. When I briefed our art department on the project, they nearly fell over. The art department team also saw the opportunity for them to showcase their great value in such a huge, new undertaking. Nobody had done this in our industry before.

There was another party in the advertising world I wanted to impress with these maps, and that was the advertising agencies. I remember getting the first full city sets of maps showing all the drug stores, major food stores, junior department stores, and major department stores by FSA. It was overwhelming. When the maps were all laid side by side, they literally showed that large cities such as Calgary, Edmonton, Vancouver, Ottawa, and Montreal were total major retail battle grounds. It was a dogfight each week to capture female and family shoppers.

One meeting with an advertising agency with which I had not done a lot of business stands out. A room full of media buyers showed up for the meeting and I briefed them on the competitive nature of the target markets for families with children and how to reach these customers in major cities. I presented the maps and spread them all over the board room table. I could not believe the reaction. The buyers in the room were totally glued to the maps. The room was silent. They could see all of the drug stores next to the department stores, and next to the food stores. At one point, one of the buyers grabbed a map and ran out of the room exclaiming, "I have to have a copy of this map now!"

It was a great year for our magazine. I grew the revenue in my territory big time that year. It was an impressive bonus payout year.

Lessons learned. Research is only good if it is meaningful to the client. Research has to be robust enough to be a market mover. Research must be really accurate or it loses all of its mojo. Timely research that gives a client a competitive edge, even for a short period of time, will move buyers to book orders right away. Corporate customers know that competitive advantages have an effective, but measured lifespan.

Please pause. Think about my research example above. Now, think about your own business vertical. What exciting research is emerging that you can bring to your corporate customers? How will this research be market-moving and meaningful to them?

20

SWOT CORPORATE COMPETITORS

Preparation for a major sales prospecting presentation involving large-budget contracts cuts a wider swath. Not only do you need to have a great proposal in hand with brilliant creative options, you also need to be prepared for a feisty battle with competitors. Competitors are always on the lookout to expand their position with your potential customers.

A thorough SWOT (strengths, weaknesses, opportunities, and threats) analysis of your competitors' position in your industry often yields great ideas for your upcoming key customer presentations. By looking at your competitor's strengths/opportunities and weaknesses/threats, you will identify the gaps between your offerings. This will help you gain the upper hand and grow your share of business with major corporate customers.

To begin, you must gather every piece of available information on your competitors through industry analysis, quarterly stock market reports, business blogs, articles, and, of course, your competitor's websites. This sounds like a huge undertaking, but with robust search engine capabilities and crafty queries, you'd be surprised what you can gather with a few stealthy clicks.

There is no perfect place to start a SWOT analysis, but I prefer to know as much as possible about my competitor's strengths/opportunities, also known as "Key Leverage Points." Competitors will almost always base their proposals on key leverage points, highlighting their unique product and service offerings in the marketplace. I want to know these key leverage points before I stand in front of a frosty customer, who may use my competitor's offerings as a tool to dampen or diminish my proposal.

Competitors' key leverage points (strengths/opportunities) may include:

1. New product development

2. New technology

3. New markets

4. Strategic alliances

5. Cutting-edge research

6. Innovative test results

7. Flexible packaging and delivery

8. And…great pricing

By understanding competitor key leverage point data, you will be able to adjust your proposal to address the above issues in a way that becomes a game-changer for your potential large corporate customer. The customer will, no doubt, respect the amount of time you have taken to analyze and anticipate their key needs and, thereby, reduce the anxiety of supplier changes.

Next, you need to know all about your competitors' weaknesses/threats, also known as "Business Implications." By understanding your competitors' daily worries, you can strategically weave this intelligence into your proposals to your potential major client and, thus, to your advantage.

Notable business implications (weaknesses/threats) to look for will include:

1. Geographical gaps

2. Technology glitches

3. Misaligned market offerings

4. Quality performance

5. Supply chain bottlenecks

6. Staffing/union problems

7. Senior management stability

8. Storage/delivery reliability and tracking

9. Problem resolution response times… to mention a few

When you are able to effectively bundle a 360-degree analysis of your competitors through a SWOT analysis, you are able to plan for most corporate customer queries during a sales presentation. Your mission is to respond with quick, crisp competitor alternatives in a live presentation setting and following up this action with inspired objection handling value statements such as:

"We hear what you are saying."

"We have been monitoring these events in the market."

"We appreciate your interest and concerns."

"Speaking of which, here is a great solution and opportunity we have developed."

"We look forward to sharing it with you and your team of experts for seamless implementation."

"This is why our customers continue to call us first, because we develop creative solutions. We anticipate critical needs."

Lessons learned. Be smart. Work to capture more than your share of your prospective customer's available expenditures. Power SWOT your competitors so you can focus more on the customer's needs while producing creative, revenue-winning proposals.

21

TURNING A DISASTER INTO A COMPETITIVE ADVANTAGE

As the FSI (Free Standing Insert) Manager for the Southam/Hollinger daily and weekly newspaper group, I was quite accustomed to receiving panic calls from any of our 125 newspaper markets across Canada. The crazier our insert business became, the more in demand I became. Incoming left-field calls were frequent and were usually managed in a phone call or two.

One day in the fall of 1996, out of the blue, I got a call from the *Edmonton Journal* EMC (Extended Market Coverage) flyer delivery service; it was appropriately named the Edmonton Flyer Force. The Flyer Force delivered inserts to non-*Edmonton Journal* subscribers on a weekly basis. Regular subscribers of the *Edmonton Journal* received their inserts in the news-paper on a daily basis. The two systems essentially delivered inserts to all open-access apartments and homes in the City of Edmonton, Alberta and surrounding communities.

The call I received was from the Edmonton Flyer Force General Manager (GM). The call started with, "Pat, we have a problem out here in Edmonton and I want to pick your brain. The problem we are having is so big and important, we just don't know what to do." As I was listening to this gent, I was thinking to myself, the tone of this call was way over the top. It was too ominous. Nothing is that grave. Seriously, it sounded like someone had just kidnapped one of his employees.

I listened and paused and said, "Okay, lay it out for me. What could be this bad?" He said, "Pat, we have Edmonton Flyer Force non-subscribers who have been calling our office and saying, we don't want flyers anymore." I understood his concern because this meant that his revenue base would be affected, and when revenues drop, operational costs must also drop. I told him to keep a file of these DO NOT DELIVER (DND) dwellings. I said to him, "We will monitor it over time and take appropriate action when it hits a tipping point. How many DND dwellings are we talking about? Are we talking about a few hundred, a thousand, how many?"

There was dead silence on the other end of the phone for what felt like forever. He said in what seemed like a very quiet voice, "There are 33,000 DO NOT DELIVER requests. Even worse, many of them are just plain blunt and even rude. Some people were even saying that if the Flyer Force did not respect their request for DND, they would take meaningful action with the authorities in Edmonton." You have to understand that there were more than 300,000+ homes and apartments in Edmonton at the time. This meant about 10% of all Edmonton Flyer Force FSI deliveries wanted a cease and desist. This gent was not just concerned, he was worried about his whole business model and its future.

Patrick Tinney

To be honest, for a minute or so, my head was spinning. I was trying to think about how we were going to explain this DND problem in Edmonton. I was concerned about how our major flyer customers would react to any plausible explanation about the DNDs. I asked the Flyer Force GM what the major reasons were for the delivery cancellations. It turned out that more and more people were moving to Edmonton for the growing oil field operations jobs in Alberta. These same people were buying and renting homes and apartments, but also had secondary accommodations in the oil patch far from Edmonton. These workers would work there for weeks at a time in the oil patch and return to their homes in Edmonton. The larger problem was that these work rotations were not always predictable. The other major group, who were requesting DNDs, were executives who were travelling back and forth to Texas. Texas is where many oil and gas head offices resided. All of this meant that inserts were not being taken in by homeowners and were stacking up at their front doors, making them prime targets for burglars. Talk about a problem.

I asked the GM how the Edmonton Flyer Force was keeping this massive list of DNDs straight and up to date. The GM said, "At first, we started making lists and sending them out to the delivery managers. The lists, however, got so long we loaded them all into a database so we could eliminate tons of paperwork and satisfy unhappy customers." This was a "eureka moment" and I said, "Holy cow, you don't have a problem at all." The GM replied, "What the heck are you talking about? I am drowning in falling revenue and what could be a total collapse of our business once our major customers find out." I asked whether our competitors were keeping the same type of database file on DNDs. He indicated that his competitors were not sophisticated. These competitors were just carpet bombing the market with flyers regardless of the DND customer requests.

Sitting at my desk, letting this flow over me, I thought, wow, what a competitive advantage! Our sales professionals can now approach all of our

84

existing insert customers and tell them that we have just figured out how to save them money on printing runs in Edmonton. We could approach our competitors' customers and share the same information. Also, we could verify them by geographical areas and now save them important budget as well. It was a potential bonanza, and the database the GM had built for insert DNDs was proprietary information. This meant that we owned this data and were under no obligation to share it with our competitors. Once I explained my observation and plan to the GM, he was almost giddy. He had the best problem of any insert delivery manager in Canada. We consequently made maximum use of this data and converted more new customers to our delivery service in Edmonton than you can imagine.

Lessons Learned. The moral of this story is that when you are in major account management and have been bombed with tons of exploding lemons, think carefully and open up a lemonade factory, and start printing money.

22

GREEN CORPORATE SALES MINDSET

As a corporate sales professional, I believe that one of the best mindsets to have is that of being green. We must keep telling ourselves that we are green and fertile. Why? There are several reasons, so let's unpack a few.

1)   **Company Product Launches**. When I was in corporate sales, I had a "me first" attitude when it came to product launches, but not in a selfish way. I wanted to be the first to test and sell products. I wanted to be the first to take great new ideas to my large corporate customers so they could have a head start on their competitors. By thinking green, I had to work out kinks and work around problems as I was testing the product myself. The idea was to remove as much risk as I could for my customer. Once I had done this homework, I could calculate the risk in percentage terms and present it to my customer as a positive risk or a "no touch." No touch means that this product is not good for you and I have tested it on your behalf.

2)   **Competitors**. Thinking with a green mindset with your competitor's product and product launches allows you to rest easy or take immediate action. If your competitor just discovered the equivalent of water or fire, you have to move quickly. We either build a case to defend our product equivalent to the competition or we better move fast to build our own product to block the competitor. That means doing a ton of homework with boots on the ground research and customer feedback. Take it from me, thinking green and fertile has kept me in the loop when others in my industry were sleeping.

3)   **Legislative Changes**. The minute a local or federal government makes a decision that will change your industry, get your green thinking going. Read all of the government white papers and decisions on how they got to the new legislation. Why, you might ask? What if you are a plastics producer right now? Are you nervous? You should be because your product category is under the microscope. You will need to remain in constant touch with the market and government. I heard recently that micro-plastics are now in our food and drinking water. Single-use straws are being outlawed. Single-use cutlery, bottles, and plates are soon to follow. If you are in this business, you had better start to think about retooling before your customers disappear.

4)   **Innovation**. Change and innovation are in lock step with point #3. For instance, many fast food companies are switching to paper straws that are crazy expensive at the moment, but will come down in price. Other fast food companies are creating cup lids that are drinker friendly. This means that the cup's contents don't spill all over the place as they are being consumed. Wear-once clothing must also go. This fabric is filling our dump sites and is not reusable. Look out for lower cost hemp clothing. Hemp clothing will decompose in landfills when it is no longer of use.

Just think about the innovative ways our healthcare products and therapies are changing. Opioids are under the microscope, and hemp CBDs (cannabidiol) are on the rise to effectively deal with pain. This is revolutionary. It is so cutting-edge that many hospitals do not even have written policies on the use of CBDs. This is crazy because people in pain are using CBDs to help offset the use of opioids. Change? You bet! The question is: will your thinking be green and fertile enough to offer amazing solutions to your customers? Furthermore, will you have the ability to provide your customers with fact-driven research and evidence that will make your green thinking invaluable.

5) **Up-cycling**. Think about points #3 and #4, and think about saying them to your customer. Imagine this conversation with a client: "After we manufacture this product we're producing, your customers can safely use it and bury it in their garden as healthy compost." Just imagine your customers' response.

6) **Efficiencies & Price Reductions**. Any time you as a sales professional can walk up to a customer and say, "I have just discovered a way to save you costs in pricing, shipping, and waste," they will leap over the table to get at you. I wrote a lesson earlier in this book titled, "Turning a Disaster into a Competitive Advantage" I urge you to re-read it. Think about how you are going to handle these types of situations in the future. I was on my game and in full green mode when this situation occurred. We made truckloads of money with the solution I recommended to my company stakeholders and new customers.

7) **Finally**. Anytime your customer is launching a product or charitable initiative, think green. How can your company help your customer drive sales with your brand inventiveness? Working and collaborating with your customer on an initiative that is important to them will make you a first-call supplier. Bring ideas to their new initiative launches and you will be treated as an insider. How much better could it be than that?

Lessons Learned. Be a green, fertile thinker. Reap the rewards. Your customers will love you for your green awareness and inventiveness.

23

WHY CUSTOMER WAREHOUSE AND STORE CHECKS MATTER

If you want to gain the deepest respect from your corporate customers, visit their stores and production facilities far and near. Visit their newest store openings. Be with them as your customers advance and live their corporate growth dream.

When I worked in corporate sales, I would make a point of setting time aside in my busy schedule to do major homework on how my customers were operating. I would take notice of everything. I wanted to know about store signage, merchandise displays, artistic approaches to product display, merchandise, in-house and branded products, licensed store partners, food counters, and so on. Even warehousing matters in some retail models because, in many cases, they are "just in time" warehouses. This means that merchandise is moved on to the floor when needed and is up to the minute. Walmart and Canadian Tire in Canada are excellent at this and, believe me, they have it down to a total science.

Doing store checks is an art form. Depending on the retailer, I would call head office and ask them which new store openings I should follow and attend. Sometimes, I would do drop-in store checks while on the road and just announce myself as I entered the store. I did this so that sales professionals on the floor would not think I was a customer and waste their time. Finally, when I was travelling across Canada and the United States, I would set time aside on business trips or even vacations to see new store formats and emerging retailers. This was important because if I noticed a new retail format in the U.S., I could inform my Canadian retailers that they should prepare for new competition. U.S. retail models, in many cases, make their way to Canada.

My old boss, Don Fisher, was a master at store checks. He was a former President at Simmons Mattress Company, so, he would literally flip furniture around to see who made some models. He also wanted to know where and how they were made. I have to say that, in the beginning, visiting a department store or a jumbo furniture retailer such as Leon's in Canada, using Don's approach would give me the willies. My discomfort aside, I soon came to understand that the staff and managers at the stores totally understood and appreciated the detail of our store checks.

At times, I would ask if the store manager was available for a quick walk around her/his store to get their vantage point on the economics of their market and how the store was doing. Demographics and store peak traffic were always points of interest for me. Retail is now a science. It is also a beautiful art form. Finally, retail is a living entity. If you listen closely enough, there is a hum in a busy department store. I love the cash register sound at checkout.

Nothing is better than returning from a store check locally and on the road, followed by a coffee or appointment with a major customer. They love to get a supplier's vantage point on what they are doing. They want to know how you were welcomed into their stores and how the employee engagement went. These days, retail sales professionals are called "associates" in some retail environments. In many stores, there are engagement protocols and the corporate folks want to know how on-the-ball their folks were.

You see, as a supplier visiting a customer's store and presenting yourself as both a customer and a research person, you are given greater status by your customers. Your customer realizes that you are taking a huge extra step to try to think as they do. In thinking like them, you have a much better understanding of their pressure points. You begin to understand how their competitors are positioning themselves to battle your other important corporate customers. All of this feeds into your presentation and proposals. It feeds into your storytelling with them about their world. In the end, you breathe their rarified air. It is then that you are invited to special coffee meetings. You are invited at their request into quiet places to discuss business ideas they have; not just stuff you are pushing across the table.

Nevertheless, ask yourself, are you just selling stuff? Or, are you exchanging collaborative ideas with your customers over coffee, talking about their world in their language? I can tell you what matters to them. If you are not sure, ask them.

Lessons Learned. Now, think about your business vertical. How are you going to employ this type of thinking? It may require a different approach, but the more you can think and breathe like your large corporate customers, the more they will appreciate you. This advanced style of thinking is what moves you up the corporate expenditure food chain, given that you are offering exceptional value to corporate customers in your business vertical.

24

CORPORATE SALES AND NEGOTIATION TRAINING

When you read the title of this piece, you might think to yourself, "Pat is talking to his sales training business sales funnel." What you have to understand is that I was in your business for about three decades, and I continue to be in your business via *www.centroidmarketing.com*.

This will always be about you. I try to keep myself in good condition and walk a mile or two every day as a way to see opportunities and work out solutions to challenges. It is how I get my brain to have a meeting with itself. The challenge is that I am the only one who can make this happen. It sounds weird, but nothing happens without me taking the initiative. The same goes for you in sales and negotiation training.

If you've been following me, you know that I did not stop going to college and university until I was well into my 30s. Why? The reason is that there were holes in my education that needed to be filled in order for me to complete my business skill sets. I always wanted to compete above my belt weight and I believe I accomplished this. Nonetheless, it did not stop there.

You see, I came to understand through some unsavory lessons in the corporate world that, if I wanted to compete at the top quintile of my sales vertical, I had to make it happen. Case in point: I realized that my world in the late 1990s would be seriously impacted by databases that were growing in power and complexity. This meant I had to have a look under the hood of these beasts if I was going to sound intelligent in front of customers. I approached my boss and asked for some training in databases, as it was directly attached to my role as Insert Distribution Sales Manager. I was the only person in this role and it made sense that I understood how the data I was selling worked. Unfortunately, it didn't happen. My boss told me to focus on selling and not on analytics/database research. He further stated, "There will be no budget for you to pursue this training need."

You can only imagine my disbelief. I do not put up with this kind of school yard logic. I proceeded to dig into my pockets. I found a database trainer to help me learn a database training program dedicated to my particular needs. My training covered about six weeks. By then, I was ready to build my own functioning flat files. I now understood what was under the hood of database construction and functionality. I was ready "to crush it" in my sales role. I did the same thing with public speaking and presentation skills. I dug into my own pockets to get these sales skills. No one could stop me, and I was determined to succeed. I read books that provided a better life for my family and made me a top quintile seller.

Knowledge truly is power. "Those that read really do lead."

Of the first six smaller companies I sold for in the media business, only one of them offered a half-day sales training program. Think about that. If I had not studied advertising in college and done a couple of short college job placements, where the heck would I have learned to sell?

During my sales career at the Toronto Star, Southam, Hollinger, and CanWest newspaper corporations, I was only placed in three good sales training programs in 27 years. I encourage all businesses large and small to take the time to seek out excellent sales and negotiation trainers who will work with you to reach your specific sales training goals to increase revenue.

If you do not get proper sales training and intend to stay in corporate sales, you will be at a disadvantage unless you are some kind of sales savant. Corporate sales are different than small business sales. The pressure to produce is amazing because so many jobs ride on corporate sales professionals meeting or beating revenue budgets. In the corporate world, everyone is watching you. I can only remember one time in my life when my sales director could not tell me whether I was up or down with my sales performance. I can tell you with great honesty that I lost a lot of respect for him for this lack of caring. My thinking is that if you are going to run me through a sales wringer washer every day, the very least you can do is track my hard work.

If you want to be in the winner's circle in the corporate world, it is up to you. You have to approach your management team and ask them for sales and negotiation training. If there is no training budget, ask them to buy you the best sales and negotiation books in the market. Next, highlight the heck out of these books. Place everything you learn on the table. Rank this new learning by revenue potential. Put the best you have learned into play. You cannot become great unless you are willing to embrace positive risk with new sales skills.

If there is no money for sales books or sales training at your company, you may be working for the wrong company. My final words to you are if you want to be the best in the world at sales, you have to think of yourself as a professional athlete. Do you think golf professionals take lessons? Yep. I can only think of one or two PGA players who think they can train themselves. Not surprisingly, they are not in the top 10 in the world. Think about that. The very best in the world of golf need training or they will just make less money. The same goes for sales. I was speaking to a sales training colleague recently. He dedicates 10% of his total income to further his sales and negotiation training knowledge base. This is what he does for a living. He is a professional sales and negotiation content producer and trainer. Please pause and think about that.

Lessons Learned. If you want to be the best, you must invest in yourself!

25

BE A GENERALIZED CORPORATE SPECIALIST

Your corporate sales education will define you at different times in your career. This means you must take some time and map out how you are going to create a point of difference (POD) for your personal corporate brand.

Your primary, college, or university education, to a degree, just teaches you how to level up. This helps you to embrace the education that will keep you in demand in the corporate sales world. Here are some stories and examples of how my POD impacted those around me.

On one occasion, I was engaged by my sales manager at the **Toronto Star** while studying the Certified Print Production Practitioner program (CPPP) offered by the Institute of Canadian Advertising. My boss wanted to know why all of the other up and coming sales professionals at the **Star** were studying marketing while I was the loner studying production. He wondered when I would be leaving the **Star** to join a printing firm.

My answer was simple. I wanted to know all about production so I could explain production problems to my customers when their advertisements were not printed perfectly, or if the colour was wrong. My manager went into a tirade saying, "We have the best production people in the country working at the **Star**. When I have a production problem, I just call upstairs to the production department to get their best explanation for the problem." He continued by saying, "I call the client and explain what production had outlined as the cause." I paused and listened until he had finished and asked him a small question. "Do you actually believe the folks in production? I say this because I don't." We stared at each other in dead silence for well over a minute and our meeting ended quietly. I had just dropped a grenade in his lap and walked out of his office.

This production knowledge would later lead me into product experimentation and development at both the **Toronto Star** and later in my 22 years at Southam, Hollinger, and CanWest media companies. In the years to come, I would launch a plethora of products. I understood the insert distribution business so well that I was known as "The Guru" for a period of time. This made me a specialized generalist not only in the eyes of my peers, but also through the lens of my customers and my company production specialists.

When I would visit our production facilities, I arrived with a handful of questions about how we could help production and how they could help us. It also allowed me to get into the weeds around where money could be made and/or saved under the right conditions. There is a certain cool feeling that goes with this knowledge all the way around the company.

Three other skill sets that added to my specialized generalist direction included participating in strategic planning, logic, and public speaking programs.

Strategic planning is a truly beautiful business practice to understand. Strategic planning allows you to peel away layers of the past, present, and future of your company. It allows you to look forward with glowing eyes. You come to visualize great possibilities, and it also allows you to lift up the hood of your company and look at your problem areas from a bare-bones perspective. It is an exciting time and one that will lead you to an understanding of your customers' product launches and your own product development in the years to come. Strategic planning is truly exciting. Please wrap your head around it if you are in corporate sales.

Some of the most difficult questions we will encounter in our corporate and personal lives begin with the word, "Why?" An understanding of logic helps us make sense of or categorize questions that almost defy all we know about the world we live in. I studied logic on a whim in university. The course name was "Persuasion in Advertising". I think the professors knew that if they listed their course as "Logic", the lecture hall stood a chance of being filled with empty seats. Bless the professors that duped me because logic has helped me so many times in my career that I cannot begin to tell you. When you combine logic with models such as a SWOT analysis, you have a huge combo tool to wield. Invite the study of logic into your life if you have the courage to face possible failure.

For those of us in corporate selling, participating in a public speaking course is a bit of a no- brainer. Still, many in sales do not like to give public speeches or even speak in front of a dozen of their peers, let alone customers. It has to do with the fear of failure and rejection. Since we all have to give large corporate presentations in large-account selling, why not give public speaking a whirl?

Lessons learned. What I have shared above is my case for becoming a generalized specialist. Before you become one, however, make sure you are a great seller and negotiator. Dig into your wildest dreams and become a generalized specialist. Take it from me, it made me money. It also separated me from my peers and my competitors, giving me a huge career advantage.

26

BECOMING AN INDUSTRY EXPERT IN CORPORATE SALES

I don't believe most sales professionals start out wanting to become an industry expert. When you think about it, it is such a daunting idea that it just overwhelms. The question becomes: why would you want to put yourself out there, only to have those who participate in your industry place you under a microscope?

For me, it was a gradual process that evolved as my industry evolved.

While working in the newspaper industry, it became apparent to me that our core revenue-generating product on-page advertising, a.k.a. run of press (ROP), was starting to lose steam. ROP was being supplanted by free standing inserts (FSIs). Inserts became the new base of consumer communication by many of our major advertisers. As a sales professional on the Retail Team at Southam Newspapers, I was right up to my arm pits in inserts. I say arm pits because the large food and department stores were the first big users of inserts (also called flyers).

The problem for the daily newspaper industry was that it did not own the insert/flyer business category outright. The dailies were fiercely challenged by weekly newspapers and door-to-door delivery services. These smaller delivery companies saw the bonanza of flyer delivery revenue. We knew the fight was on. The only difference for us was that flyers were cannibalizing our ROP on-page advertising business.

Understanding that I could not change the ROP shift to flyers, I started to turn my attention to defending our flyer turf. In doing so, I wanted to know how much profit we generated delivering flyers through our daily newspapers. My solution was to develop an in-house survey for our 16 daily newspapers to complete. Once returned to me, I could aggregate the survey findings and share it with our company newspapers.

The findings from the newspapers and from other data I had collected were eye-opening and game-changing. We realized that we had to learn more about flyers and fast. We realized one more thing. We were all selling this emerging flyer product differently. This caused confusion for us and our customers. You see, our on-page advertising was universally sold by "the line." A full page was comprised of approximately 3,000 lines of newspaper advertising space at the time. Flyers had no boundaries and our delivery of flyers had no geographical consistency. It was like "The Wild West."

As a head office sales professional, I was always looking for ways to build templates, systems, and languages that everyone in the company could identify with and use. After speaking to my flyer professionals across our newspaper group, it was clear to me that there was no single strategy or language that was emerging to sell flyers. That is why I set out to address this issue. We needed a model everyone in our daily newspaper group could use. It had to include quantities by geographical delivery areas, maps, colour coding, insert machine specifications, and shipping specifications. Once completed, I shared my draft model with my boss, Don. He asked, "Why are you doing this?" He said, "Pat we have professionals from across the country that do this one function all day, every day. What makes you think you can teach them anything? I think you are in over your head." I didn't agree with Don and finished the model for all of our newspapers. I created the first ever "Southam Newspaper Guide for Selling Flyer Distribution". Once I sent the more than 20-+page guide out to the group, they loved it and started adopting it.

In the end, my research and development work on the single-language model for selling flyers became the national industry standard. I imagine "The Guide for Selling Flyer Distribution" is still in use today. Only now, the guide will reside in a digital format and, hopefully, have been further improved.

The good news is my insert/flyer research only intensified in the years to come. I spent about another decade growing this business category before departing the newspaper business altogether. By then, I had tested, standardized, and launched numerous flyer distribution products. In this process, I uncovered revenue streams that my company could not have dreamed of years earlier. In the middle of my tenure as the Flyer Distribution Sales Manager for Southam, Hollinger, and CanWest, I also became a Founding Director of the Flyer Distribution Standards Association of Canada.

Lessons Learned. Becoming an industry expert in corporate sales was both rewarding and challenging. It definitely opened doors for me, but has not defined my career. For me, the best is always yet to come.

If becoming an industry expert is what you aspire to, I recommend you make sure it is a business category that you truly love and can live with for a long period of time. Almost nothing in business stays the same. Change is baked into the business cake.

27

STRETCH IN CORPORATE SALES

"Stretch," in this case, is not what you are thinking about in corporate sales. While working for the Southam Newspaper Group, I was given an opportunity to participate in the first of its kind "Pricing Strategy Committee." Our company pulled in managers, directors, and even a president of a division to join the committee. This meant that we had representation from right across Canada in all areas of newspaper advertising departments and complimenting business divisions.

Our mission was to pull apart all we knew about our businesses to see if we could find improvement for revenue growth and profitability. It was an amazing challenge and everyone on the committee knew we had to produce some constructive findings to help drive revenue and report our findings to the executive team. Therefore, producing a bunch of fluffy, nothing burger results and resolutions was just not going to cut it.

After our first meeting, we decided to call in experts in the world of media pricing. We needed their global take on how conventional media was pricing itself right across the world. In essence, we wanted to know what rabbit holes to avoid on pricing and what innovative avenues would be worth pursuing. Did we ever learn what to avoid? For me, it was listening to the impact of conjunctive, bulk annual contracts and the negative results produced by media companies that implemented them. The word "damaging" comes to mind. When you bill at one constant low rate for all business from a single business partner or agent, you get severe margin compression. We quickly decided that this was a pothole and confirmed with our executives that it would never work for Southam Newspapers. The evidence was overwhelming.

Owing to my gearhead sense of curiosity, I got involved in our insert distribution business. The company had a sense it was profitable in this business category. That said, no one had deconstructed how all of the costs were calculated in our insert business including labour, machinery, systems, and union agreements in place. I thought the best way to get at this was to visit some of our distribution sites and do a company-wide survey of how our machinery worked. Next, I constructed what I thought was a pretty doable survey for our newspapers to fill in and reply to with their individual notes. What I had not taken into account was the size of the output. I was and still am a spreadsheet/database enthusiast. The problem was, I had no idea how big this data would become. The term "Holy Cow" comes to mind.

I ended up with so many spreadsheets that, when all of the results were tabulated, I had a 100-+page legal-sized deck of mouse type. To manage this, I decided to tack all of the spreadsheets up on the walls of our boardroom in rows all around the room. When I finished, I just stood there in awe. I am pretty sure I was talking to myself about how one tackles something this big. My general manager walks in. He looked at all of the spreadsheets and he looked at me. He said, "What's up Pat?" I looked back at him and said, "This is huge. I know I will figure it out, but this is going to take time." His reply was simple. "Don't look for things that match. Look for anomalies."

I am confident that I would have eventually figured out this enormous jigsaw puzzle. Regardless, my GM nailed it with his observation about this size of data. Look for anomalies—and I did. Another colleague walked into the boardroom and addressed me, having heard around the office what I had created with this insert/flyer survey. Unfortunately, he had less than compelling observations to offer. He couldn't think as big as I could. He tried to cut me up. Not a chance. I knew I was holding an enormous opportunity.

A VP visited one of our meetings with all of our pricing committee members in attendance. He queried my survey results and asked me, in very crude terms, "What the frick I thought I was doing?" Also, he continued, "Did I not think the company knew how it made money?" The room was in shock. Dead silence. I just looked back at the VP and said, "Actually, I don't think you really do understand how you make money." He was infuriated. Our committee members all just stared at him as if to say, "Pat's right." Shortly after, we presented our findings to Southam's advertising operating committee (Advertising VPs). The Advertising VPs loved their new understanding of our business in total, but also their understanding of their own local insert business.

With the findings we had all participated in building, our newspaper executives could now go back and look for even more efficiencies. The world has changed a great deal since I produced this insert survey report. It was my opportunity to stretch. It was my approach to understanding our insert business that changed the way I looked at our company going forward. As a matter of fact, I would say that this stretch experience is what gave me the deep belief in myself to launch bigger and bolder products for the company and its future owners. Equally important, it opened my eyes to even greater possibilities for more innovative customer revenue: growth proposals. The whole pricing committee experience really stretched my confidence in both IQ and EQ terms.

Lessons Learned. If you are working in corporate sales and you get a chance to work on a company-wide committee that you think has great future meaning, consider the opportunity carefully. It could be just the stretch that will enhance your entire sales career.

PART III – RELATIONSHIPS & TRUST

28

CORPORATE DINING ENTERTAINMENT TIPS

Nobody enjoyed putting on epic lunches and dinners more than I. Great clients such as Steve Cosic, Greg Crombie, and so many others got the royal treatment when I was entertaining. We ate at the best restaurants and enjoyed the best wines I could dig out of their wine cellars. Visualize the ambiance, storytelling, and laughter as you read on.

Entertaining important corporate clients in a dinner or formal lunch setting is an art form. Food is so common, yet so complex. We all have to eat, but how each of us interprets food is totally different. When you add culture into the mix, you have yet another notable dimension. On top of this, many people these days have more food allergies and sensitivities than they did in past decades.

Coming back to culture, you must take into account that there are just fewer than 200 countries in the world. The major culinary influences in the world come from China, France, Japan, Italy, Thailand, India, Spain, Mexico, and American stylings.

When you entertain clients, you want them to enjoy and be comfortable in a dining environment, versus a trend point in culinary artistry. Understanding if your customer prefers a formal or informal dining setting is critical to a successful and memorable meal. None of us has the right to tell someone else what to enjoy. Therefore, if you feel you do not already have an idea of their preferences, make the effort and ask the right questions.

There is one more element to add to this mix and that is dining etiquette in the Western world. Etiquette, some will agree has been lost, but should not be forgotten. It is not uncommon for business professionals who have accumulated great wealth to be unaware of how to correctly hold a knife and fork, never mind a flotilla of spoons, forks, and knives associated with "fine dining, white linen service." Business dining should be taken seriously. Take the time to read about and practice appropriate table manners and social graces.

Here are several tips to consider when entertaining a new customer in a foody environment.

Clients' dietary needs- preferences. Increasingly, dietary needs and preferences are coming to the fore in client entertaining. For example, I have a friend who is deathly allergic to fish. Every time we dine, I go to great lengths to inform our server that fish must not touch the cooking surface on which my friend's food is being cooked. If so, he will become seriously ill and must be rushed to the hospital immediately. None of these important details can be overlooked if you want to have a great dining experience with an important client. Do your homework.

The dining experience. Dining should be fun, relaxing, wonderfully paced, comforting, and, above all, well beyond the prospective client's expectation. Make it so. Work with your restaurant team and plan where you will all sit to enjoy the visual experience of the restaurant, as well as its ambiance. Extra tip. If your client is a "Foody", see if the chef will visit your table to check on your dining experience. Some Chefs are great with customers and this personal conversation lends itself to a great memory.

Reconnaissance. I like to scope out a restaurant before inviting big corporate clients to dine. Go online and read restaurant reviews. Ask colleagues for referrals and recommendations. Find out what a restaurant specializes in. Visit the restaurant at peak periods to make sure it is well staffed. Read their food and wine menus. Visualize where you would like to sit with your client so you can speak quietly and intently. Be smart and get in behind the restaurant battle lines. One more thing: this may sound petty, but check out their rest rooms. If the bathrooms are grungy, you can only imagine what the conditions are like in the kitchen. Note to self.

Business goals. There is a lot on the line in gaining a new corporate client; therefore, it is important to have business goals you look to achieve during a dining event. In many cases, you can accomplish these goals without it even sounding like a business meeting. Make no mistake about achieving your ranked goals before you leave the restaurant. This will ensure you've covered all that you intended during this meeting. This will also underscore the importance you place on your client's time and business objectives.

Plan questions. When I am in a dining setting, as with all client meetings, I always pack questions that are ranked based on their financial importance. I call them "money questions" because if not answered, I may be leaving money on the table for a sales competitor.

Plan concern- objection responses. Corporate clients will not buy in a negative risk environment. Every business category has challenges it must face. All businesses have competitors, and the market never rests. Make sure you are up to date on your new client's concerns in your business category. Be prepared to listen to them and supply them with information to address their concerns.

Plan trial closes. I love trial closes because, as a sales professional, I can trial close all day long with prospective clients and not offend them. An example of a trial close is "What is holding you back from buying our products and services?" If the answer is "Nothing really", the client may actually ask you to deliver the first order, just with an innocent query. The trick is to plan at least five or six carefully crafted trial closes. Rank them for efficacy and timing during and leading up to the end of your dining engagement.

Day, time & location. Ask for your client's input on where it is most convenient to meet you. They may even have a favourite restaurant where they get preferred seating and service. You must ask the questions or miss an opportunity to please your corporate client.

Menu/beverages. My son cooked for a decade professionally for one of the world's largest hotel chains. I enjoy cooking and used to be a junior wine collector. SO WHAT? There are many executives in the business world who don't know or care about delicious food and great wine. If you are one of these food agnostics, approach the restaurant and ask the chef to help you plan the menu. The proprietor and chef will be more than pleased to offer advice on food, wine, and other beverage pairings. When you take this extra step, you look professional. More importantly, it will signal to your corporate client that you care about their dining pleasure. This detail could be a signal to them that you will care equally about their business.

Conversely, if your client is well travelled and a wine connoisseur, solicit their input before making the restaurant selection. Once the location is selected, contact the owner or chef to discuss fine or rare wine pairings to match the acclaimed menu.

Transportation safety. With drinking and driving laws in place, it is important to make sure your corporate client has only consumed what the law allows. If this element of your dining entertaining is in doubt, prearrange a car service or taxi to ensure they arrive home safely.

Lessons Learned. My old friend Steve Cosic frequently said, "Pat, the devil is in the details." That said, so much can be gained for a sales professional who goes out of his/her way to turn food into a lifelong memory. Years after leaving The Bay, Steve Cosic would relive our most amazing food outings as if they happened yesterday. Building trust and much needed personal relationships is based on anticipating needs and deeds that exceed expectations.

29

CLIENT PROBLEM RESOLUTION

If you ask any seasoned corporate sales professional or sales manager about their worst client product problem or total malfunction, they will sit back in their chair and pause for thought. Some may cringe. Others may place their hands over their faces. We all know in business that customer mistakes and delivery problems are going to happen. It's just a matter of when it occurs and what we do to fix the problem. Other variables include speed, quality, satisfaction, and, in some cases, compensation.

Speed matters. If something goes wrong or is about to go wrong with a client delivery of product, I advise that you call the client before they find out. Why? The answer is found in your integrity. The answer also lies in the client's belief that you will help them fix the problem. This means that you will get them back up and running as quickly as possible.

You also have to consider the scale of the client incident. There is one more element. If the problem happens in a geographical region and you in sales are dealing with a customer head office, you have two calls to make. Call your head office client quickly, so they can call their regional contact to reassure them a problem has occurred and will be resolved quickly. The other instant call is to your regional operation to let them know to call their local contact so that everyone is in the loop and working together on their behalf.

Scale. The scale of any client problem with one of our products is critical. The bigger the problem, the more resources we have to bring to bear to help our client partner. Creativity comes into play as well. I will offer up more on creatively solving problems later in *The Bonus Round*.

Coordinated Communication. When a corporate customer problem happens and customer regions are involved, a totally coordinated approach to communication will bring down the level of angst that includes our regional people. It means all parties are involved in a satisfying solution. Our boots on the ground matter. Reassuring regional customers matters. I cannot emphasis this enough.

Satisfaction. When something goes wrong with the deliverables of a product or service we have sold to a customer, make sure the customer feels good about the value of the solution we offer to them. I know this may sound obvious, but it is not. I am about to outline a creative solution I used to solve a crazy, persistent customer problem. Customer satisfaction matters. If you lose a customer because they were not satisfied with a sales solution to a sales execution problem, I say your sales organization has a larger problem.

Let me share a short true story. While working at the Toronto Star as a sales professional, I landed a music store account that specialized in pianos. It was never going to be a big account because it was a single-store location in a modest setting. As a teenager, I worked for a retailer that sold Yamaha pianos. My music background made me feel confident I could help this customer sell more pianos.

The *Star* had just introduced a solid, new advertising section that ran on Saturdays at a deeply reduced line rate. The reduced line rate was applied because we pushed copy and art deadlines forward by a week. With this extra time, we pre-printed the product called "Showcase". It was perfect for small businesses such as my piano store client.

The piano store ran on-page advertisements in Showcase for several weeks in a row. The ads worked wonderfully, selling all kinds of pianos for the owner. The ads were modest and usually featured two or three different styles of pianos. The pianos included upright pianos, studio models, and small furniture models with front legs to support the keyboard. On the fourth week, somehow a leg on the furniture piano was broken and it was displayed when the advertisement ran. This broken leg was surprising because we had an ad proof showing the piano in its normal state. The customer was ticked off, despite the fact that piano sales were going well. After much negotiation, I convinced my management team to rerun the modest piano ad at no cost. Problem solved. Everyone was happy and we booked a new round of advertisements.

Things got weirder. Every second advertisement we ran for the piano store showed a piano with a broken leg, even though I was now processing complete one-piece art to avoid the initial problem. I would even go upstairs to the production department to check the piano ads before they went on press. My relationship with the piano owner became strained. I just could not explain the crazy broken leg scenario, which played out month in and month out.

Another problem developed because my management team tracked our profit on this account and began to refuse "make good" compensation. This was my solution. I told the piano store manager it would be wrong to discontinue the advertisements because they were driving great sales for his store in spite of the broken legs on the pianos. I told him that we would start an accumulative credit account for him. I explained to him that, after every fourth ad with a broken leg, I could justify a complete make good on one advertisement. It became a broken leg incentive plan.

In my entire career in newspaper sales, I have never experienced anything like this and have not since. The only logical explanation was that someone in the production department had it in for the piano store. I am convinced of this because none of my other accounts were affected. This was crazy.

Lessons Learned. Customers are so hard to come by that they must be cherished and protected. We must stand by our customers through thick and thin. We must remain profitable or we will go broke solving problems that will not go away. When the going gets tough, the tough get creative. Finally, work extra hard for your customer when execution becomes an issue.

30

RELATIONSHIPS MATTER

If you have read one of my other two sales books, you may be familiar with this career-altering story. I must tell you, there are times when there is a macro-story that is not always clear, but reveals itself years later. In the lesson that follows this lesson, I put the whole story behind the story in plain view when you read these two stanzas in tandem. Here we go. Buckle up!

A group of buyers I trained a while ago asked me the following questions: "Are relationships really needed, or should I be harsher in business negotiations? Am I exposed if I have a relationship with a corporate sales negotiation partner?"

These queries underline the pressure and tumult that buyers face in the uncertainty of our current economic conditions. Buyers start to second guess their core business beliefs and values in an effort to excel at the bargaining table.

As long as buyers are respectful and have a degree of empathy for their corporate seller negotiation partners, acting firmly or weakly is just part of the dance. Compressing or decompressing time is just an everyday tactic used in a negotiation.

There are dozens of tactics and strategies that professional buyers use in negotiations to unbalance the seller. The buyer's job is to move the seller off their script quickly so the buyer can start asking armour-piercing questions for which the seller may not be prepared. This helps pull the corporate seller closer to the buyer's negotiation objectives.

We must not, however, leave our bargaining partners unfulfilled by a negotiation. Sellers that feel like they have been "taken to the cleaners" may start to resent a negotiated deal. Once resentment sets in, the deal will start leaking oil. Problems that inevitably pop up may not be handled well, placing the contract fulfillment at risk.

Solving problems is just part of business life. Notwithstanding, solving a problem for someone with whom we have a positive, trusting relationship will get greater attention. It's more than just a problem; it is a creative process to try and help a friend in need.

At the end of a multi-million dollar contract negotiation with one of Canada's largest department stores, I made a mistake in a very quick verbal exchange with a buyer. It was an honest misunderstanding. It meant that our side would end up banking hundreds of thousands of incentive dollars that my buyer would not know about until we were very deep into the contract.

I was really happy to have signed the contract ending a long multi-million dollar negotiation, but as I started to recount the mistaken exchange on the way back to the office, I knew I had a huge problem. Approaching my sales manager at the time, I explained the situation. He told me not to worry and just wait for time to expose the problem, and we'd deal with it.

This didn't sit right with me. I knew this was a career-defining moment. I went for a very long walk in six inches of snow for about an hour. The more I thought about the mistake, the more I was convinced that letting this problem fester was all wrong. Trust is so hard to build with an important customer and I could not put my interests in front of my client partner's interests. With my sales manager's reluctant blessing, I set up another meeting with my buyer. I exposed the mistake and extended my apologies. The buyer quietly mulled the situation over for a minute. He asked me to correct the mistake in the contract so he could sign it. He also told me that my quick action clearly saved him a lot of budgeting grief later in the contract. Problem solved. End of story. Well, not quite.

Years later, our company changed ownership and was embroiled in a painful restructuring. Many jobs at my firm were lost in restructuring and there were stories in the news about more to come. My phone rang at the office. It was the same department store buyer mentioned above. He asked me how I was doing and was there any uncertainty around my future. He told me not to worry. He explained that he had already started making calls on my behalf and that if my job was lost, I would be working within days with his industry influence. Corporate negotiation relationships matter.

As a buyer, I would rather have a negotiation relationship with the seller than not. My reasoning is simple. I am responsible for how much the other side knows about the inner workings of my company. In this, my exposure is measured and calculated.

My goal is to reduce negative risk and raise positive risk with information sharing. As partners, we move toward positive two-way communication. I do this to pull them closer to my buyer negotiation objectives. Ultimately, this will strengthen the relationship and raise the spectrum of getting a long-lasting, smart deal done.

Lessons Learned. I recently polled some seller colleagues about being treated harshly or being commoditized at the negotiation table. Almost all the sellers had a similar response: "Do I take my best creative ideas to a buyer with whom I have a good relationship? Or, do I turn to someone who thinks nothing of my company and has taken advantage of me?"

The seller group was not filled with alacrity about the notion of sharing great ideas with negotiation users and abusers. Corporate negotiation relationships do indeed matter.

31

THE STORY BEHIND THE STORY

If you have read my earlier content or my sales books, you'll know that my largest account was the Hudson's Bay Company while working in the corporate media space. The last iteration of the series of media companies I worked for was CanWest. CanWest was a globe-trotting broadcast company before it purchased my employer Hollinger Inc. for $3.6 Billion, making CanWest one of the largest media companies in the world.

The Hudson's Bay Company was one of the oldest companies in North America and was born as a fur trading company in Canada in 1670. The Bay, as we called it, owned Zellers, Canada's largest junior department store, and a couple of other large retail brands. In media spend terms, the Bay was a juggernaut with an annual media budget of approximately $100 Million in the mid-1990s when I was active with the account. In the early 1990s, I was presenting $12–13 Million-dollar incentive plans to my friend

Steve Cosic, who was soon to become AVP Media Procurement for the Bay and its other interests.

I believe I had the largest retail portfolio in our company at that time, reaching $35+ Million. I worked on some very complex Pan-Canadian accounts. The pressure was large. Account responsibilities of this magnitude have the sales account custodian on high alert 24/7.

The challenge for both Steve and me was that from a 50,000-foot view, our fortunes were tied together. Our ideal customers were a combination of females, families with children, and those with mid to better income. The other challenge we both had was that our senior management teams kept getting rolled over with each team becoming meaner and uglier than the last.

On the CanWest side, our new owners "managed out" the long-standing senior management team. CanWest did this to bring in a new senior management team from within CanWest and from outside media companies from the United States. The testosterone floating around in our buildings was over the top. I remember being called to the first meeting of the new CanWest/U.S. senior management team, only to have our new President of media bellow, "If you do not fricken well like it here, leave. We do not want you!" He was addressing about 300 media managers, account managers, and support staff. To be honest, I thought it was hilarious and told the new president so. Three quarterly meetings later, the new president was still bellowing the same message and you could feel the blood draining out of the company. Believe it or not, the next senior management iteration was even wilder. I finally parted ways with the company after 22 years of continuous sales and sales management service. I was a bit of an iron man.

On Steve's side, he had the same deal. Management teams just kept rolling over, only to be replaced by another group of street fighters. Parts of his company were under the microscope. The consumer was starting to gaze toward the Internet, but those were still baby-step days for Internet shopping.

For everyone in retail, the problem was that fashion had lost its way. To make matters worse, "Wealthy Boomers needed less stuff and were spending more money on travel and fixing up their homes." Canadians were starting to take on debt that would eventually make the U.S. debt per capita look like the pregame warm-up here in Canada.

Canadians were buying more and bigger homes and condos. Simultaneously, rents were starting to rise at an alarming rate. Finally, the Generation X, Y, and, eventually, Z crowd were not loyal to department stores let alone shopping centers. There was change in the air and it was weighing on department stores sales results.

I was in the Bay's flagship store at Yonge and Queen Street in Toronto and ran into Steve Cosic's new boss and VP of Marketing, Neil Fedun. Neil was about 6 feet 6 inches tall and had a huge handlebar mustache. Neil was just steaming through the middle of the main floor and I greeted him. I said, "Hey Neil. Great to see you. How are you doing?" He replied, while blowing past me, "Don't ask me how I am. Buy something for God's sake." Yikes. Neil left the Bay not long after this in 2002. This meant that Steve was now reporting to the executive team and the pressure just got bigger and bigger.

Both Steve Cosic and I timed our departures from the corporate world well. Steve was bought out and pensioned off. I was lucky enough to get all my pension money out of the company just before all of the HR departments called staff in from all over the country to tell everyone the bad news. "The pension fund was breaking down and it could get worse from here." In fact, it did get much worse.

Lessons Learned. Take care of your dream corporate customers. They need you. Many will step up to defend you in your hour of need and when you least expect it, as my dear friend Steve Cosic did.

I believe in destiny. After I left the company, I had an epiphany. I was driving up a highway near our head office. My gut went off. I put in a call to the benefits department of my ex-employer. To my amazement, they picked up the phone. I told them that I had a question and asked if I was allowed back in the building. They said, "Sure. Meet you in the cafeteria." We sat together and I asked them one simple question, "I know my pension money is not indexed, but how much will it grow over the next 20 years until I need it?" They replied, "Your pension is now frozen and will not grow a penny." I knew that by just putting this money in the bank, it would grow by at least 2 to 3% a year. I asked, "How quickly can you write a check for the proceeds of my pension?" They replied, "Fast." I said, "Cash me out." I received a check for my pension in short order and I ran to my bank and told them to cash this check as quickly as possible. There was something still bothering my gut. About a week after I cashed this check, the HR departments at my ex-employer broke the news at each newspaper about the pension collapse. I think I may have been one of the very last to get my pension money out and into the safety of my bank.

32

ARE YOU LIVING YOUR CORPORATE BRAND?

Are you living your corporate brand? It sounds like an awkward question, but for most in large account management it shouldn't be. It should be our "Why". It is our reason for being. I wish more sales professionals would think more about this question, as it shapes how we view the world in business in the present and future.

I have always been proud to wear any of my employers' golf shirts, jackets, etc. No problem. The big element in living your company brand goes way beyond wearing a piece of clothing with a logo on it. Since our customers are both external and internal, I thought I would share a couple of examples of living my corporate brand.

In Toronto, we have an organization for retailers and media people to meet called the Retail Advertising Club (RAC). On a yearly basis, the RAC holds its annual meeting and awards ceremony. One of the categories that advertisers and advertising agencies compete in is Free Standing Inserts (FSIs), and, more specifically, insert creativity and effectiveness. Any winner of one of these awards would be over the moon. To have an advertising agency win is really big because these awards attract new clients. Every retailer wants to be associated with the top winning advertising agency in their category.

About two days before the RAC Awards entry deadline, I received a call from Greg Crombie, CEO of Building No. 4 Marketing. Greg is a long-time friend and wanted to land one of these awards. He asked if I (the National Insert Manager for the Hollinger Newspaper Group) would look at his RAC submissions. I said, "Sure, send them to me right away and I will work on them now." I knew time was super close. I read Greg's submissions in three insert categories and they were excellent, as one would expect from a marketer of his caliber. What I saw were a bunch of small, tidy-ups that would add colour and flavour to Greg's submissions, to give them a story-line that would resonate with the judges. Greg was thrilled with my recommendations, and our hope was that one of the three submissions had a shot at a win.

I was unable to attend the RAC gala, so, when I got a call from Greg the next day, I nearly fell off my chair. Greg and his agency had won in every category they entered. The chances of this happening were plainly remote. The two of us old friends laughed our backsides off. More importantly, it brought our close relationship even closer. I was a supplier who pulled one of my important friends into the winner's circle when he wanted to rise up in the important insert business category. To me, this was living my corporate brand big time, and I know that Greg's buttons were busting for weeks.

(Sadly, we lost Greg to cancer about a year or so after he won these awards. I miss Greg dearly. He was and still is a friend's friend.)

By 1995, I had logged about nine years with The Retail Team at Southam/Hollinger. The newspaper group had been fun, but I needed a change. I wanted some national advertising agency exposure. I believed I could achieve this if I landed a sales position with one of our national magazines. A posting went up for a sales role with a magazine and where I knew and liked the gang there. It looked like a great fit for me.

Just as I was getting ready to apply for the magazine sales position with my boss's blessing, my coordinator, Jack, walked into my office. Jack asked me if we could have a quiet word. No problem. Jack is an amazing person. He worked so hard for me and the team that it would be an honour to help him in any way I could, business or personal.

Jack said that he loved working for the retail team, but he needed a new challenge. I agreed. Smart. He said, "I am applying for the national magazine sales position." I paused for a moment. I was trying to think about how to address my friend. I said, "Jack, you are making a great decision. It is time for you to grow. There is one challenge for you. I am applying for the same role." Jack looked at me as if I had just shot his dog. He said something to the effect of "I can't beat you, so…" I said, "Jack, not so fast. We are going to get you ready to interview for this position and I am going to prepare you so well that there will be a decent chance that you can win the role." Jack looked at me as if I had lost my marbles. He just sat there and pondered what I had said. He asked, "Why would you do this? Why would you prepare me to try to beat you?" Again, I thought carefully. I said, "Jack, as my coordinator, I want you to represent my best efforts and that can only happen if you are more than prepared to beat me. Secondly, there are sales jobs that come up all the time in the company. Think of it this way, if either one of us misses the national magazine sales role, we will be extra ready for the next sales opportunity. Finally, it is smart to interview for sales roles periodically to keep your interviewing skills sharp." To be honest, I just could not do this any other way. It might sound odd, but the right thing to do does not always mean we win at all costs, at least not in my world.

Jack must have interviewed for the national magazine sales job brilliantly because he was a different person afterward. He had a deep sense of calmness and peace. I eventually accepted the magazine sales role, but the interviewing process ignited Jack. When the next magazine role came up in the company, Jack nailed it. He was so successful that he next became a publisher, and a young one at that. Afterward, Jack just kept rolling up so many magazine and personal business achievements that it was hard to keep up with him. Jack is brilliant.

Lessons Learned. My advice to all senior sales professionals and managers is to promote your people if you can. Holding people back for personal gain is weak. You heard me, "Weak." If those that you promoted enjoyed working with you, they will be in your lane for years to come. These great sales professionals will always be open to a conversation or, perhaps, even offer to help you. You see, living your corporate brand is much more than a grab bag full of logoed material. Sure, I was proud to wear my company merchandise. I am even more proud, though, that in my corporate sales role, I was able to make a big difference in the lives of others. Be strong, be brave, and show integrity. You will be remembered for it.

33

HOW TO BE A TRUE NORTH MENTOR

Having someone mentor or coach you at any time in your life is a seriously great opportunity. It means that someone senior has taken an interest in your career growth. It also means that they are trying to listen to your concerns and ambitions, while sharing their experience and expertise.

I had some very bad mentoring as a lad. Thankfully, that scenario improved as I moved through my career. I am blessed to have had some guardian angels looking over my shoulders at just the right time in life, and, specifically, in my business life. In real life, I can name a few colleagues and mature business friends who were just standouts. I hung on every word of wisdom these mentors shared.

Jeff Jarvis, Chairman of the Applied Arts Department at Sheridan College in Oakville, Ontario, was a mentor during my college student days and onward. Jeff always had a ready ear and a generous vision of my future. I remember, one day, I hitchhiked to college from Hamilton, Ontario some 20 miles from home, with no money for lunch. Jeff noticed I was sitting in a reading room when all of my classmates were eating in the college cafe. He questioned me and I reluctantly shared my situation. Without hesitation, he reached into his pocket, handed me $10.00 and told me to go have lunch. The next day, when I returned to college and offered to pay him back, he refused. He did force me, though, to make a promise. He said, "Pat, going forward if you see someone down on their luck, you must give them this $10.00." When I relayed this story in a eulogy on Jeff's passing, I mentioned to the congregation at the church that this promise had cost me thousands of dollars. The church attendees roared with laughter and nodded. Jeff was a mentor in the most profound way. He really cared and I know I appreciated all of his wisdom. What a great friend. What a gentleman.

Bob Hillier, Don Fisher, and Stan Shortt have all been great business mentors over my corporate sales career. Each one of these gents revealed parts of the business world that I would have not been exposed to if not for their kindness. Each of them answered my endless questions. If any of you have spent any time with me, you know I am a question person. Bless Bob, Don, and Stan for being great friends and for their amazing guidance.

In college, I never saw myself as a leader or mentor. I was just a survivor. Yet, at a lunch about five years ago, a college friend laid out the situations where I had mentored her when it was not apparent to me. It only goes to show that you never know who is listening to you and why.

I have been blessed to mentor some amazing people, to help them grow their sales and negotiation games. At times, it was just helping them identify their strengths. It doesn't matter what the subject material entails. What does matter is that you listen as a mentor when someone is really going through a growth spurt or an unexpected blockage. Both business scenarios matter because we all have our ups and downs. It's not a question of how many times we fall, it just matters that we get back up. Good mentors expect this and are there to reassure us. When our careers are swimming, it is great to have a mentor at hand who can help us maximize unique opportunities. Remember, corporate sales careers are not forever. We must be diligent about getting the most out of every stage of our lives.

If you are not a mentor, I recommend you take some time and think about the positive impact you could have on someone's future. I did not come from an active business family. Much of what I learned about "behind the curtain business activities" happened as a result of a mentor pointing me in the right direction. Will mentoring always be a breeze? Not a chance. Remember, you become a mentor to help someone in need in a low self-interest manner. You are not mentoring to receive a mindless trophy. The cool thing is that many sales professionals you will mentor will find their intended way. This exploration process can take years, and patience is a must. Success is a process, not a race.

If you are seeking a corporate sales mentor, choose carefully. There are businesspeople who will appear in your life and act like mentors, but they do not have the empathy or low self-interest to fill this important role. Some sales managers like to groom newer businesspeople, to carry their water. Beware and choose carefully. I can tell you from my own experience that some who act like mentors will take you to the cleaners. It happened to me.

Lessons Learned. If you search for a mentor with true-north self-awareness, you will find your own Jeff, Bob, Don, and Stan. Mentors, both male and female, are waiting to help you. They will share their vast experience and knowledge openly. Trust yourself and your true north mentor. Believe and dream big. Dreams do come true.

PART IV – GETTING DEALS DONE

34

CHANGE THE RULES

Years ago, Zellers was Canada's largest junior department store. They were also a 52-times-a-year FSI (Free Standing Insert) advertiser. Canada Post was Zellers insert/flyer delivery service, but elected to move out of that business vertical. Canada Post left Zellers to buy into new insert/flyer delivery systems across Canada. Most of these Zellers inserts found a new delivery system pretty quickly. The competition to close out a "whale-sized account" such as Zellers was fierce.

In one particular Ontario market, Kitchener/Waterloo, the battle for the Zellers flyer contract turned into a total dog fight. My employer owned the **Kitchener/Waterloo Record** daily newspaper. There were two other capable flyer delivery services in Kitchener at the time. This meant our newspaper was not a shoe-in to win the business. In Canada, the flyer business is a commoditized sales service. Selling anything that is a commodity can be just plain ugly because competitors are basically selling an identical offering. In our case, we had the advantage of having the *K/W Record* as the flyer carrier for our subscriber homes and apartments. Our subscriber offering was excellent, but did not reach the whole city. We also supplemented our delivery of flyers with an EMC (extended market coverage) door-to-door service. Our EMC was matched with our subscriber delivery address list, so there was no duplication of delivery. Our competitors were a bulk, door-to-door delivery service, meaning they had no paid subscribers. One might assume that having a subscriber-based delivery service would give us a huge advantage in this square-off for the Zellers flyer account, but not so. Our two flyer delivery competitors were also the two largest commercial printers in Canada. Thus, you can only imagine what value-added was embedded in their proposals.

The pressure to close out on the Zellers deal was immense. In the flyer business, once a contract has been awarded, it takes months and, sometimes, years to move a contract again. This means that nailing down the flyer contract at the first opportunity is critical. The proposals that were being presented to Zellers by our competitors must have been eye-popping because our claimed subscriber advantage was not holding water. The sales and management team at the **K/W Record** were doing all they could locally to sway this business, but the business was not sliding to our side of the margin in spite of our very competitively priced proposal. Kitchener was one of the last markets in Canada to settle. Most of the other markets were being locked down with firm proposals. I know this to be true because I was the sales professional/manager on the account. It was clear that once I signed this Pan-Canadian contract with Zellers, it would be the single largest flyer contract ever penned in our company history.

The management team at the **K/W Record** had done their part selling to the Zellers local store managers. They were looking to me to close this deal out and fast. This deal represented approximately $250,000 in incremental revenue to the **K/W Record**. As each day passed, the calls from the management team at the **Record** got more intense and more frequent. My calls to the Zellers' head office buyer team turned up with the same intensity. Everyone was edgy. To make matters worse, my head office management team started breathing down my neck. The **K/W Record** team was pounding on the table and, to be totally honest, everyone had a right to their stated position. We were all staring at the same puzzle. We needed a game changer.

Part of my deep interest in flyers was not only in the sales side of the business; I was intensely interested in the circulation and distribution side of it as well. This is where Sandy MacLeod (**K/W Record** Circulation Director) played a huge role in a revised Zellers/**K/W Record** proposal.

In one of our Zellers and **K/W Record** conference calls, it became clear to everyone that we needed to change the rules of the proposal game to which we were all committed. As we entered an intense part of the call, we were looking for ways to leverage our strengths and expose our competitors' weaknesses. The wild cards for all three parties in the bid process for the Zellers' business was access to all apartment buildings in Kitchener/Waterloo. This meant a greater understanding was required about which of these three competitors was doing the best job delivering to the rural areas surrounding Kitchener/Waterloo. Finally, the topic of measurement came to the fore. Sandy MacLeod held the keys to the answers to all three of these questions.

With $250,000 on the line, Sandy and his circulation team took on the task of surveying all apartment building owners and superintendents. Sandy's team surveyed to find out who had access to each and every apartment building in Kitchener/Waterloo. His team also completed audits of the rural areas around Kitchener/Waterloo. The circulation team did this to confirm how each of the three distributors matched up in terms of flyer delivery quantity and quality. It was a major undertaking with investment involved, but it was so important. With all of this information in our hands, we could compare this data to detailed Canada Post home and apartment counts by city and town. With this report completed, there would be no question as to which distribution company was delivering as they had promised.

In the end, the survey of detailed dwelling counts was the deal clincher. Sandy MacLeod's circulation team struck deals with as many apartment developers as possible. They did this to gain door-to-door access to apartments because, as subscriber delivery agents, we already had access to these same apartment buildings. Where apartment door-to-door access was not available, flyer lobby drops were set up and were monitored. Sandy's team did this so that superintendents did not have to recycle unused flyers. In some cases, for practical purposes, we just hired superintendents to be our delivery agents for their apartment buildings. This added nicely to their income.

Our competitors could not match our home delivery in and out of the city and could not match our partnerships with apartment owners. We matched up two last pieces of data that cinched everything for us. We compared the detailed Canada Post housing counts and the vacancy rates within the city to arrive at a net delivery number for the entire community of Kitchener/Waterloo. This benefited Zellers big time. It meant they would not over-print flyers and offered them one more quality level of assurance that the **K/W Record** would be Zellers' flyer distribution partner for many years to come. We changed the rules to win the game.

Lessons Learned. Some of the very best customer proposal ideas happen when everyone is exhausted. Read Tim Hurson's book, ***Think Better: An Innovator's Guide to Productive Thinking***, to learn more about exhaustion creativity. Remember to SWOT your company and your competitors in all tough deals, especially in commodity-based deals. I did not use the acronym SWOT in this lesson, but it is implied and helped expose our creative winning proposal. To learn more about SWOT for your company and your competitors, read ***Unlocking Yes, the Revised Edition*** and ***Perpetual Hunger*** by yours truly. Finally, rules are just rules; they are not laws. Rules are meant to be examined and interpreted. In some cases, rules are meant to be broken. Change the rules.

35

OPPORTUNITY SALES OBJECTIONS

Preface: This is a special note. An objection, concern, or worry from a corporate client can block a sale. Please remember, just because someone is not pounding the table with an ugly objection, it does not mean the sales process will move forward. Where big corporate money is concerned, it is all about risk and profound exposure in the client's mind. This is why digging out concerns or worries is such an important function of pulling whale-sized deals across the finish line. Now, let's dig into opportunity sales objections more deeply.

Opportunity objections in a corporate sale or negotiation are the gateway to truly understanding what the customer really believes and wants. An opportunity sales objection is also what is standing between us and a great sale of a proposal. An opportunity objection is a blockage to a converted customer who is happy with a sale and the purchase they are about to make.

If there are no objections in a sale, we as salespeople have become nothing more than clerks writing orders that have absolutely no stretch or positive risk associated with them. In other words, we are managing transactions of commoditized products.

Most salespeople do not practice handling customer concerns or objections. They try to manage this process by thinking on their feet. By doing so, they are counterpunching with customers packed with personal anxiety, and using phases such as "We've already thought of that." This does not take the customer's worries away, but rather shelves them. To a degree, it makes the customer look uneducated for asking a legitimate question with potential personal exposure. Making the customer feel dumb is not a great way to close a sale or build a much-needed relationship.

Here is the way to succeed with opportunity concerns, worries, or objections.

1)   **Listen.** If a customer raises a concern or worry, he/she is doing so to mitigate risk. Listening intensely to our customers is paramount. Don't interrupt. As a customer, if I get the sense my salesperson does not care about my risk, I will slow down the sales process until I feel the risk is in check, or worse, just walk away.

2)   **Rephrase.** By rephrasing the customer's concern or worry, we as salespeople have acknowledged there is a potential blocker to a sale that must be addressed. It also means that we are getting a clearer sense of the customer's objectives.

3)   **Empathy.** Letting the customer know we empathize with their worry or concern brings us closer to them. It's a relationship builder. It's a trust builder. No amount of money in the world can buy trust. It must be earned and protected.

4)   **Query.** Asking well-crafted, high-value questions will get to the bottom of most concerns. The worry could be safety, financial, or past bad experiences. We must uncover the nature of the concern to have any hope of neutralizing it. If this blockage is resolved, the sales process can move forward.

5)   **Creative solutions.** Now that we have a better understanding of our customer's worry by asking great high-value questions, we can set to work our ability to reshape the offer or proposal to fit the customer's eye. Think scale, innovation, service, quality, delivery timelines, and payment plans. Leave price as a last resort and use it only if we are profitable.

6)   **Collaboration.** Openly solving problems with a customer is the pinnacle of consultative selling. It signals that the customer and salesperson are opening up their minds to arrive at a greater good and fulfillment for both. Collaboration is actually "the green shoot" of a future and profitable negotiation.

7)   **Our POD.** Our ability to truly express our "Point of Difference" at this stage of solving opportunity objections is what will separate us from our competitors. Our POD also has the ability to reduce commoditization.

8)   **Benefits.** When addressing an opportunity objection and having explored the core of the customer's concerns or needs with an array of solutions, we are now able to talk about benefits.   Not just any benefits. They must connect us emotionally to the customer. They must make them feel safer, more creative, smarter, more efficient, relaxed, and less exposed. Think of these benefits as benefits on steroids.

9)   **Trial close.** If, as a top-level salesperson, we have guided our concerned customer through her/his opportunity objection using the above process, we are ready and the customer is primed for a trial close. See if the

sales process can now be closed with a question such as "Valued customer, when and where would you like to begin to enjoy this great program?"

Lessons Learned. As you handle a concern, worry, or objection from a corporate client, make sure you make it to the trial close of this concern so you can put the sales process back on firm footing. If you can get a buy-in with a trial close, you are back on track with an important corporate customer. In bigger deals, there are lots of mini-deals that act as building blocks to landing whale-sized deals. Think in detail, with a process. Think end to end.

36

THE CREDIT DEPARTMENT CHANGED ME

If you bring up the credit department with the average sales professional, they will give you a polite smile, but I imagine many are in their deepest heart of hearts thinking, please don't touch my accounts. Don't speak to my accounts. Don't even think about my accounts. On the bright side, I have never seen a sales professional walk into a credit department wearing a garlic necklace or chanting religious verses to save their accounts' souls.

Seriously, when I first accepted a role in sales at a community newspaper with a compensation plan that was comprised of a church mouse's salary base and a modest commission plan, my life was tied at the hip to the credit department. The reasoning was simple. If I sold advertisements, I got paid a commission. If my customers did not pay their bills, the credit department would claw back my commissions. Consequently, I would be left sucking air, blaming everyone but myself for not carefully qualifying the account.

Yep, you heard me correctly. Ultimately, the loss of commission was my fault for not doing my job in understanding my account's financial health.

I imagine that what I have laid out above sounds fair and reasonable. Now, I want to fast-forward you to a large corporate account sales setting, with an understanding that $Millions and $Millions of dollars are being sold by responsible account professionals. At the same time, equally responsible credit professionals are monitoring cash flows from our customers to match the amount being sold. In other words, in business, we do not want more money going out than coming in. When this happens, account professionals can expect a polite note from the credit department saying something to the effect of "Account X owes $1.5 Million past 60 days." Now, depending on the size of account, this may be an easy problem to solve with a few phone calls. A courier is dispatched to pick up a nice, big, juicy check from account X so we in sales can continue selling to this amazing account.

On the other hand, if account X is $1.5 Million in arrears and their annual budget is $4 Million, in my opinion, we have a three-alarm fire. All hands must be on deck so this account comes back into a positive frame so we do not have to cut them off. You read this correctly: occasionally, multi-million dollar accounts get cut off. This is why I had such a healthy relationship with the credit department. I would pick up the phone or even walk upstairs and sit with the credit folks. I would sit in the credit department and work out a repayment plan for our valued customers to keep them current with us. Having the credit department on our side in sales is very powerful. Let me share a story about when I worked for Canada's largest newspaper group.

I was the account manager on one of the largest home fashion accounts in Canada called "Family Home Fashion" (not its real name). The account had locations from coast to coast and was expanding at a breath-taking speed. One of its largest and most successful product lines was flooring; this included carpets, tiles, wall to wall, you name it. When my credit department called me, Family Home Fashion (FHF) was modestly in arrears, but I was informed that the account was booking advertisements faster than they were paying for them. This is a red flag. A couple of weeks later, I got a call saying, "We need a check to keep the account going." I said, "Sure, how big?" The voice on the other end from credit said, "$200,000++ and we need it today." You know in corporate sales that, at some point, these days are going to happen. It happens when business is crazy, but you never see yourself in this position. I said, "Okay, I will meet with the client later today and I will get as much of the $200,000++ as I can." In my mind, I was saying to myself, "This is a biggie. This is game day."

My meeting with the CMO of Family Home Fashion started off very well. We were beginning to speak about the future and how many new advertising-on-paper run of press (ROP) advertisements were coming up. I thanked her very much for the new business and said we had one more item to discuss. I mentioned that FHF's account was in arrears and, according to my credit department, I needed to collect a check today. She seemed a little taken aback. I told her that I needed $200,000++ today. In about two seconds, my request had sunk in and she just went ballistic. I listened quietly to all of her anger and protests, but said, "If I do not have the check in hand when I return to my office, FHF's account would be cut off." We would not accept any more advertising until the $200,000++ was paid. She went ballistic again, but became louder. She went nuclear. I got my check, but she told me that she was calling my boss after this outrageous meeting.

When I arrived back at the office, I was in a mad rush to get this huge check to the credit department. In the middle of my rush, I stuck my head into my General Manager's office. My GM was in a meeting with a sporty looking fellow. My boss asked how things were going. I said, "Fine. I just picked up a $200,000++ check in back payments from Family Home Fashion." He said, "Great job." I thanked him and acknowledged the gent across from him, and said to my boss, "There is a sh*t storm heading your way with my name on it." He smiled and thanked me for the heads-up.

When all of the dust had settled with my client, the credit department, and my boss, my coordinator walked into my office. He said, "Pat, just as you left this morning, about $100,000 worth of free-standing insert orders came in from FHF for next week and the inserts have already been shipped." He said, "I just got the orders in by the skin of my teeth, but we are good. How did your meeting go with FHF?" As I told my coordinator about the bombast of the day, it hit me. The reason my client went crazy was not about the money per se; it was about the millions of date-stamped inserts that were travelling on trains to my newspapers as we sat in this meeting about paying up bills. She was stuck between a rock and a hard place, but did not want me to know. I had leverage of which I was not aware. She must have thought I was some kind of clairvoyant who could read her poker tells and the stress she was under.

In the end, all turned out well. I worked with the credit department and we kept our client healthy for another day. Oh, and the fellow sitting across from my boss that day was the new VP of Advertising for the company who had just been hired and was introducing himself as my boss's new chief. I am pretty sure I made a good impression. Credit goes to credit on this one.

Lessons Learned. The pressure that comes with working with whale-sized corporate accounts is undeniable. The pressure to perform is expressed by both buyers and sellers. Monster problems are what we get paid to solve. Buyers and sellers can be great friends. In-spite of this, messy money flows happen. Over-spending happens. Businesses go bankrupt or become insolvent. This is real. Professional corporate salespeople understand this. The game is big ball. If you want to sell for as long as I did, you need to study business intensely. You need to create partnerships within your company that seem counterintuitive. My relationship with the credit team was critical to my success. I owe them a huge vote of thanks for their trust in me to be their voice in some really dicey circumstances. Trust takes a long time to build. Take the time to build trust with your credit department. Trust wins the day. Remember, a sale is not a sale unless you get paid.

Oh, BTW (by the way), the $200,000++ figure was not the real number. I will say that it was the largest check I had ever picked up from a client for being in arears. Think about this. I was in the corporate sales business for 27+ years. The check I picked up was so big, it vibrated.

37

CREATIVITY WINS THE DAY

If you know anything about Canada, it is that almost all of our major cities are attached to water and, more specifically, rivers. As new people from Europe arrived in Canada in our early history, settlers needed fresh water to drink. Settlers also needed to water their livestock so cities sprung up around rivers. Winnipeg, Manitoba is one such city.

When I was a corporate account manager at Southam Newspapers, we launched a door-to-door insert/flyer delivery company called the Flyer Force. The *Winnipeg Free Press* was the newspaper of record at the time and carried most of the inserts. The *Free Press* delivered to paid subscribers, box/store sales, and they had a non-subscriber delivery program, meaning, they were trying to blanket the city.

The Southam-owned Winnipeg Flyer Force was launched in Winnipeg as a competitor to the *Free Press*. It was comprised of a number of community newspapers as carriers of news and flyers. At the time, we were working really hard to fill delivery holes that the *Winnipeg Free Press* had not attended. Thus, our door-to-door delivery numbers were not only competitive, they were impressive in their completeness when compared to total city dwelling counts. The Winnipeg Flyer Force quality of delivery was on the money. Our pricing was more than competitive.

I was having great success selling the Winnipeg Flyer Force and was converting lots of small to mid-sized corporate accounts. I was building a base that Canadian major and junior department stores would have to notice. Specifically, I focused on the junior department store category. I zeroed in on Woolco stores as a conversion target. Woolco stores were the predecessor of Walmart Canada. Woolco had five+ stores in Winnipeg and they all seemed to be somewhat satisfied with the *Winnipeg Free Press* flyer delivery. There really was not an alternative until we launched the Flyer Force and started to rack up all kinds of new corporate clients.

I presented the Winnipeg Flyer Force to Woolco media buyer, Fred Roy. In spite of my best efforts, though, I could not convey the superiority of our delivery systems. The Flyer Force's general manager was Randy Blair. Randy was, and still is, one of the sharpest business operators that I have ever worked with. Randy worked with the Woolco store managers locally. I continued to listen to Fred's needs at the corporate offices. I presented plenty of appetizing proposals, but with no sign of movement.

Randy and I discussed endlessly about how to move Woolco. We decided that what we were doing was not dramatic enough. Woolco was a giant 52-times yearly flyer and on-page advertiser. If we could convert Woolco, it would create $400,000+ in incremental revenue. It would be the largest sale for the Winnipeg Flyer Force to date. The pressure was on. We had to convince Fred Roy to visit Winnipeg. Fred needed to observe the river bridge systems in the city. Fred also needed to understand the consumer flyer delivery challenges impacting his stores and how we were solving these problems.

Fred finally agreed to add Winnipeg to his business travel schedule, but we needed to punctuate our Winnipeg Flyer Force delivery superiority. We decided that we had to get Fred in the air. He needed to see how our delivery system and the rivers all played a part in how human traffic made its way to his stores. At first, we talked about renting a hot air balloon to show Fred the city, but Randy's idea of renting a small plane hit the mark. Once in the air flying over Winnipeg, Fred could see how our delivery system could do what the *Free Press* could not. Human traffic flow and rivers were impacting his stores. I have never been involved in a deal that closed with a flight over a city, but in this case it worked far better than anything we had tried. A 10,000-foot view was the creative closer to move Woolco.

Lesson Learned. When you are working hard to impress a client conversion sale, place everything at your disposal on the table. Work to understand your key leverage points. Make sure you are presenting the right business case. Build the right story. Convey the impact that your products and services are having on the markets you serve. The story may have to be told from a 10,000-foot vantage point. Give your creative ideas wings to fly. Creativity wins the day.

38

SELLING VIA MOBILE, ZOOM, SKYPE, OR EMAIL

Increasingly, the business community is breaking away from face-to-face corporate sales and negotiation, and choosing to move these critical engagements to mobile calls, Zoom, Skype, or email. When we strip away the ability to make direct eye contact with a corporate buying partner, we lose one of most valuable EQ measurement tools. When we cannot see all of the person's body movements or cannot reach over and touch buyers, the conversation takes on many new dynamic tones. This opens up all kinds of mine fields regarding how our motives are being viewed and interpreted by our negotiation partners. Some buyer and procurement groups are using email as a firewall or a vendor fact-checking tool. They send out RFPs (Request For Proposals) knowing that this information will be used to keep their current preferred vendors in check or, worse, under cost pressure.

We could discuss this topic at length, however, below are my 10 best tips when selling or negotiating using mobile phones, Zoom, Skype, or email:

1)   **Be proactive.** I like to be the person initiating the call to the other side. This is important, as it gives me greater time to get my ducks in order. There is nothing worse than being pulled out of a vital business engagement and, suddenly, being plunged into a different sale or negotiation. Think of how many times a corporate customer calls up with a budget they want to spend. They pull us out of another deep engagement that is eating up all of our mental and emotional energy. It takes great agility and concentration to pull oneself into the present new opportunity.

2)   **Preparation.** It is essential to prepare for this call or email in an extraordinary fashion so, if we get knocked off script or plan, we have as many tools around us as possible. Knowing our customers are accessing data bases and pulling range reports on pricing, it is vital that we keep up-to-date files on past sales and negotiation pricing with all important clients.

3)   **Ranked objectives.** There really is money in ranking our objectives before a non-face-to-face corporate sale or negotiation. If we are not fo-cused on the dollar value of each of our objectives in a ranked fashion, there is a chance that we may overlook an important objective. Note to self: clarify exactly what the other side needs, and match that information with our needs. Now, look for the opportunity gaps.

4)   **Monitor time compression.** Managing time is a beast in non-face-to-face sales and negotiations. The other side can create an at-mosphere of urgency by ratcheting up deadlines designed to force decisions quicker than normal. If you feel this type of gamesmanship is taking place, slow the process down. Call for a break on the basis that our side needs time to review our best options on our corporate partner's best behalf. This pays dividends in the long run.

5)   **Cost modeling.** I am a huge fan of cost modeling, especially for large or mercurial corporate accounts. When customers are making large

expenditures with our company, there is an expectation that we are always on top of their account. Second, if we know we are dealing with a detailed multi-level sale or negotiation, it pays to be able to shift gears between cost models on various products to come up with the best solution possible in a live setting. This is an advanced scenario. Increasingly, as more and more customers avoid face-to-face sales engagements, we will be required to make tougher, quicker decisions to hold and grow our share of a customer's budget.

6)   **Simple language.** My advice to Centroid Training clients who sell and negotiate using email, mobile phones, Zoom, or Skype is to be very careful with the words they choose. As I mentioned earlier, we cannot assess all of the body language of the person on the other side or their facial expressions as they react to our responses. Avoid any temptation to fit in a joke or a glib remark, as these actions can totally derail a constructive discussion. Stay with the facts, listen more, and speak less.

7)   **Control your emotions.** Never let them see the whites of your eyes. Even if you are anxious, frustrated, or angry, don't let the other side see or hear this. It is a sign of weakness and the other side will feed off of this misplaced emotion.

8)   **Note-taker's role.** We cannot listen, think ahead, and write with great accuracy in a fast-moving, big budget, conference call or negotiation. This is where pulling in a note-taker for the call pays off big time. The detail a note-taker can pick up is so valuable. If the note-taker is a colleague or superior, …all the better because a person at this level can also slip us notes or questions we might not have been able to get to.

9)   **Close positively, with broad agreement.** Once a sale or negotiation has closed out on all of the germane items on everyone's wish list, sign off the call positively and quit talking. One misplaced word at this point of

the proceeding could reopen the sale or negotiation. Stop. Sign off, and get working.

10)   **We control the agreement language.** The last piece of any mobile, Zoom, Skype, or email sale or negotiation is the detail in the contract. We always want to be the author of the contract if possible. It is almost impossible to get every detail in an agreement covered in a call. Be alert. Control this part of the sale or negotiation, as there will always be little details in the contract that we would prefer to craft to benefit both sides, while limiting exposure to our side.

Lessons Learned. Limit the number of potential land mines and trap doors in mobile, Zoom, Skype, or email corporate sales or negotiations. This is what top-tier corporate professionals do naturally. See the sale or negotiation from end to end before you get on the call, and expect the unexpected. Be proactive and, above all, manage risk in a constructive manner.

If you cannot get in front of a corporate customer, I recommend using a Zoom conference call. My experience is that we will just continue to expand the use of Zoom. I expect Zoom to expand the capability of its platform so it will be just like sitting in front of a client.

39

FRAMING CORPORATE SALES OR NEGOTIATIONS

When readying to engage in a face-to-face corporate sales presentation or negotiation, it is a mistake to overlook framing the proceedings. Too often, I see neophyte stressed or harried sales professionals rushing to crack open a presentation or negotiation with their corporate buyer partners without setting the stage for all at the table. It's truly a missed opportunity.

By framing the past, present, and future dealings with a corporate customer, we have a unique moment to contextualize our intentions and those of our company. In doing so, we also have an opportunity to check the temperature of the other side for their openness to cooperate and collaborate. If we don't experience cooperative feedback from our corporate buyer partners, expect a longer, thornier engagement. This last touch with the customer allows us to shift strategic and tactical gears to fit the terrain.

There are a number of ways to frame a negotiation; however, the subjects below are at the top of our list of must do's. This is our opportunity to be a storyteller of all things good about getting smart deals done that will stand the test of time.

1)   **History.** Past bargaining sessions with our corporate buyer partner can motivate the future. By speaking to the history of our two respective companies and the successes we have enjoyed, we are able to shine a light on future opportunities. If this is our first business presentation, we can elect to profile how our business category regularly conducts and concludes successful cooperative sales. The idea is to look for planks to build a solid bridge with our customer.

2)   **Common interests.** By visiting common interests with our buyer partner, we are laying even more solid planks on our bridge to a successful deal. Common interests may have both monetary and non-monetary implications. Common interests may even include potential community building and philanthropic opportunities. These community and B2C awareness programs create more mutual opportunities as an organic off-shoot.

3)   **Common objectives.** In citing common objectives with our corporate buyer partner, we are really asking a question. We are querying about closure of distance for the larger items in a sale or negotiation such as price, quality, and time —"The Big Three." If we speak to the other side about "The Big Three" and we get positive feedback, we know that entering the bargaining continuum (a.k.a., the zone of potential agreement) will be easier. If, however, we get silence or disagreement, rest assured there will be more heavy lifting to get closer to the door of a deal.

4)   **Spirit of agreement.** The spirit of agreement is really a nice way of saying "code of conduct" or "code of common courtesy." There will either be honour among men and women or there will be honour among thieves.

Whether faced with cooperative bargaining or game theory competition, it is always good to know there will be a framework for overcoming obstacles and blockages in a professional manner.

5)   **Mutual opportunity.** During the framing process, it is good to try to get a measurement for everyone to have a meaningful piece of opportunity. When framing this part of the sales presentation or negotiation, if we get a sense from the other side that the deal will be lopsided in their favour, it is time to suggest that we look at a bigger pie. By expanding the opportunity for both parties, the sales process takes shape, giving our side the incentive and fortitude to conclude a fulfilling and constructive deal.

6)   **Determination.** There is a strong correlation between momentum and determination in successfully closing a large corporate sale. When framing a large sale or negotiation, we really want to hear from the other side that they will see it through. We want to know that we will both have "puts and calls" that will need to be addressed and successfully navigated with everyone's interests taken into consideration. If, at this point, we get a limp response from the other side, we may be in trouble. If the other side is affirmative and enthusiastic, we are ready to go, and well on the way to closing another smart, accretive deal.

Lessons Learned. There may be some out there who think framing sales presentations or negotiations in a corporate buyer engagement is too theatrical and a waste of time. To those I say a deal is not a deal until the goods have been delivered and we have been paid in full. I would also say that poorly crafted deals are bound to leak oil or may be unreliable in the delivery phase. Notwithstanding, my friends, frame your deals smartly. Tell the other side they matter and that you care. Tell them everyone deserves to make a profit.

Special Note. Large corporate deals are generally watermarked by a series of smaller presentations and agreements with our corporate buyers, leading up to jumbo agreements. In this light, framing any corporate presentation is a must. Consistency in this regard makes us look even more professional.

40

INNER PEACE REVEALS CONFIDENCE

One of the things most of us cannot fake in corporate sales and negotiations is inner peace. There are a couple of ways to achieve this higher level of self-awareness and confidence. The obvious way to achieve inner peace is to do a deep work-up on our partner and their culture prior to any presentations. This is combined with cost modeling, incentive plans, back-up plans, and an eye-popping proposal delivery strategy.

There is a second way to arrive at inner peace and it will surprise many. First, build trust with those you are about to engage in a sales presentation or negotiation. Share some stories about how deals get done in your area of interest and expertise. Once this bridge has been built, share your larger vision for a deal and explain where your corporate buyer partner fits into the deal. You see, there will be times when you are selling and negotiating with multiple partners. They may not be attached to each other. They are, however, vital to the over-arching vision for a jumbo deal.

You might think that sharing a larger vision with a corporate buyer partner would reveal a weakness, but this is not so in all cases. Knowing and trusting your corporate buyer partner puts you in a position of strength to open up. The funny thing is that, by truly understanding your larger vision, your buyer partner will become enthusiastic about seeing this deal happen. Many times, they will get creative about how they can help and bring their expertise to the table. This adds even more collaborative value.

I have done this in big printing contacts where I was the buyer, and I have performed the same function in negotiations on behalf of my family where there was a lot at stake. There is an old saying: "Everyone is in for a win or a tie." In this context, share this vision of an inner peace scenario. Your corporate buyer partners may very well feed off your confident energy, especially if your buyer partner has never pulled a complicated deal together with multiple negotiation partners. In this scenario, there is both profit and learning in it for your negotiation partners, which can create some really rewarding magic.

Drew Harris, the printer partner I worked with on a print and distribution deal to deliver a free-standing flyer to over 60% of Canadian homes gets misty about that deal. Drew gets nostalgic about the enormity of the print run and the complexity of that deal. He still says, "I had to order so much paper that we had transport trucks lined up around our entire printing plant."

Nevertheless, friends, work for inner peace at the corporate buyer or seller table. This level of confidence makes all of those around you take notice. Your corporate partners will recount to their friends and customers how they worked with you on a vision that just blew them away and continues to do so to this day.

Lessons Learned. If you have trusted partners who understand that there will be profit in a deal for all, then they will open up a bit. This may be uncomfortable for some. Please understand, to build this kind of confidence and inner peace, just make sure you choose great opportunities to share with great partners. You can identify sales and procurement professionals who have done monster deals. They know how to embrace positive risk. They prepare thoroughly so they can achieve deep inner peace. You can, too.

41

EFFECTIVE TRIAL CLOSES

Special Note. Trial closes are money questions. Let me repeat. Trial closes are money questions. Please, burn this into your sales brain and master the art of the trial close. This is why we are revisiting trial closes.

At a gathering, I asked a relative in my wife's family, who once owned a large car dealership, what was the best piece of deal-closing advice he had received over his storied career. He took his time to respond and said, "Yes, I remember it well. A giant in the auto industry once told me that to be successful in car sales, I had to visualize that I was always standing in a round room." He had passed along a gem that remains with me today and a quote that I often use in our Centroid Training sessions. Metaphorically, he was saying, take the corners out of the room so you have room to back up and regroup.

Patrick Tinney

One of the themes I like to leave with our Centroid Training graduates is that nicely crafted questions delivered politely are innocuous. We can ask tons of carefully crafted questions in our pursuit of a "Yes." An example of a trial close question is, "What would it take to get this deal done?"

The alternative is to ask a question in a hard, closed-ended fashion. An example of a closed question is, "Do we have a deal?" This small question might seem like a risk-free query in the closing stages of a business deal, but it isn't. By asking this direct question, we have initiated a "coin toss" result. The answer will ultimately lead to a yes or a no. This means that by questioning in this direct manner, I've opened up a 50% chance of a "No" in the overarching sales deal. I have inadvertently backed myself into a corner by asking this question so directly.

Let's get back to visualizing that we are operating in a round room in the closing phases of a sales deal. By asking a direct question, I have senselessly built a corner where there was none. I am boxing myself in. Question? Is there an appropriate time to directly ask for the deal? Yes, there is. The time to directly ask for the deal is when you have exhausted all lower-risk trial close questions, including our examples below, and/or when you are running out of time.

Ask trial close questions similar to these examples:

1. Where would you like to begin our proposal?

2. When is the best time to initiate this proposal?

3. What about this proposal do you like, and which of your stakeholders would like it too?

4. Which group in your organization would benefit most from our proposal?

5. How do you visualize closing out this deal?

Trial closes are a thing of beauty because they do all of the heavy lifting of a direct close without boxing us in. Additionally, if we are in collaboration mode with our new customer, they may actually offer up valuable information. In a better case scenario, they actually share creative approaches that they visualize on the potential deal. The customer may even start to sell us on his/her ideas to get final closure of the deal. In the best-case scenario, they say, "You know, we've really discussed the opportunities and exposed the risk in this proposal. I think there are more positives than negatives. Let's sign this deal and get going."

Lessons Learned. Centroid Training participants learn that trial close questions are money questions and I sincerely believe this. When heading into an important sales presentation, rank your trial close questions for dollar value and effect. Think about how much time you have in an important sales proposal presentation with a senior corporate executive buyer. The answer is, not much. Craft your trial close questions carefully. Rank them. Practice them. Role play with them. The better you get at delivering trial close questions in pressure-cooker corporate sales presentation situations, the more deals you will close with the lowest amount of risk.

Book Recommendation. Beyond *Perpetual Hunger*, James Muir's *The Perfect Close: The Secret to Closing Sales* is the best trial close book in the market today. Author Muir uses a two-step trial close, and it is powerful.

42

NEVER APPEAR MORE PROSPEROUS THAN YOUR CUSTOMERS

If you are in major account sales, never appear more prosperous than your customer. Never drive a flashier car than your customer. Don't wear high-end designer suits that your customer would not wear on a daily basis. Why, you ask? Customers take very close notice of how their sales representatives present their standard of living.

I can remember, on more than one occasion, enjoying lunch with a customer when one of the customer's other sales representatives happened to be in the same restaurant and I heard the customer say under their breath, "We will have to review how much business we are doing with that rep; he/she appears to be living a better life than we are." The resentment sets in. You might think I am blowing wind with this warning, but, remember, we are all walking and talking brands. When our brand says, "Hey, look at me. I am rolling big time!", not only do your peers notice, but so do your largest corporate customers. This is a neat story for you about not appearing more prosperous than your customer.

A few years ago, I was shopping for windows for my home, and the price tag was going to take us into the $thousands of dollars. My wife was delighted, but I was less than enthusiastic. Think about it; people do not wander up and down your street comparing windows. Anyway, the last sales representative on my cattle call of window sales professionals shows up at my home, and this guy is slick. His presentation and list of value-added guarantees made him the perfect choice. There was one thing that baffled me though, so I said to him, "Enzo, you are by far the best sales representative we have engaged today. You nailed it with your presentation and offering. You are superior."

My question is, "Enzo, why are you staying with this company you are representing? They treat you horribly. You look like you are just scraping by with your beat-up old car and..." He stopped me with the wave of a hand. "Mr. Tinney, I have worked for ABC Window Co. for 25 years. I am their top salesperson. All my calls are red hot prospects and my close ratio is excellent." I had to ask, "So, why are you driving a Vega?" Enzo politely replied, "My Vega is my 'feel sorry for me' car. I actually drive a Porsche. Think about it this way mister. Would you buy windows from a guy in an expensive suit and driving a Porsche?" He had me hook, line, and sinker!

Lessons Learned. We all know the industries that culturally embrace super expensive cars and designer suits for their sales professionals. I endorse dressing professionally and driving a mid-priced brand-new car. There is nothing wrong with that. I get worried about sales professionals who are not living in their customer's shoes. Resentment is a really big problem to overcome. Note to self.

43

HOW CORPORATE SALES PROFESSIONALS CLOSE DEALS

I get totally focused once the proceedings of a corporate negotiation have been properly framed. Once we have a general agreement, the buyer and seller start moving more confidently toward closure of a mutually beneficial deal.

The closure of a large, corporate deal can happen in dozens of different ways depending on how much budget is involved and how complicated the components of a deal are. Generally, in larger deals, there is almost a cadence or process many in business will expect and recognize. It is generally not a rushed affair unless the customer makes it so. It almost has the feeling of a train starting up its engine.

When I am closing out a deal, I want to pass a series of check points and bolt down all of the pieces of the deal before the train leaves the station.

Whenever possible, I want to be the engineer of the train as it picks up speed on route to its closure and profitable destination. Here are the check points in a profitable deal closure I want you as a corporate sales professional or entrepreneur to pay extra close attention to.

Positions tabled. We always start the close of a corporate deal with all positions that have been tabled in the deal. We do this to be sure there have been no changes in the hours or days leading up to this last meeting.

Build a bridge. We lay the planks of a bridge in a deal by starting with the elements of the deal that everyone agrees on. We may even use a leading question to prompt the proceedings such as, "I think (buyer partner) that you'd agree, are we simpatico on the following list of items." We do this for two reasons. First, we get the corporate customer to say "Yes" because we want the customer to get used to saying yes. This builds much needed momentum to get the deal done. Second, if there is any hesitation, this is the moment to address it and move on with greater confidence.

Lower cost items. Next, by addressing lower cost items in the negotiation, we are building even more momentum and laying more planks on our bridge. Broad agreement at this point means that we just have one big hurdle left.

Tough stuff. The last elements of a deal almost always have to do with price, quality, and time. If we have listened clearly to our corporate customer's needs and motives, our cost modeling and the incentive elements of our proposal do the heavy lifting here. If you get bogged down a bit with the customer over sticking points, just remain calm. Act underwhelmed, as if you expected this last tactical move from the customer. Once this bump has been cleared and we have broad smiles, we start to really zero in on the close.

167

Recap. It is always wise to do a short recap of the deal just as a final touch point to make sure all major points in our proposal have been accepted in their various forms.

Ask for deal. We close by stating, "If there are no outstanding items, I believe we have a deal!"

Finish the deal on an upbeat note. Always finish positively even if the last part of the deal was a bit of a hand-wringer. Stay calm and shake hands with your customer. Smile and leave the building.

Stop selling. Why leave the building if you have a deal? Why? Simply because every extra word we speak as a seller after a deal has been closed increases the risk of unnecessarily re-opening the deal or, even worse, losing the deal. I have seen deals actually close and the seller could not stop talking. They continued to give more profit away unnecessarily and even recklessly. Note to self. Stop selling. and Leave the building.

We draft the contract. Once a deal has been struck, stop and capture the last details of your final meeting. If it is a very important corporate deal, this is where having a note-taker with you pays big time. The corporate seller always wants to be the one who drafts the contract to be signed. There is a simple reason for this. Small details that did not get covered in the deal become your responsibility. Interpret them as you remembered them, and write the details in the written contract. This is where smart sellers reduce their exposure to buyers who might want to ask for add-ons not documented in the contract. This is also the part where you may want to control the terms of payment. Everyone has their own view of what is important in these small details.

Parties sign-off. Once the contract has been drafted, it is simply a formality of getting the agreement signed and dated by both parties. Is this important? In a word, Yes. What if the person you just shook hands with on a deal gets sick or leaves the company? The contract speaks for that person in their absence and stands as a living document.

Last thoughts. If the products and services you sell are straightforward, use the pieces of the close-out process described above to best fit your business model. If your contracts are ironclad and clearly spelled out, you are in a position to ask for the sale and just close-out.

Lessons Learned. Closing-out a jumbo, corporate deal is perhaps the most exciting part of corporate sales. It promises great beginnings and profitable futures for both the buyer and seller. Pay close attention to the tips I have offered you here. Signing important contacts is like winning a game of chess. If you can do it once successfully, you can do it over and over again. This will grow your sales confidence and business profitably for many years to come.

44

WHAT IS YOUR CORPORATE SALES MANTRA?

Years ago, I decided I needed an internal sales advantage over my peers and competitors. I needed a statement that was personal, simple, and yet provided me with deep motivation every day to constructively engage customers and colleagues alike. I decided to create an easy to understand mantra.

Fast forward to a recent discussion with a young sales professional about mantras and why I felt everyone should have one. I asked him if he could work with a mantra to keep himself on top of his sales game. I shared my own mantra, which is, "Am I relevant? Do I add value?" Obviously shocked by the directness of my mantra, his jaw dropped and he said only one thing. "Man, that is cold!" I was satisfied that my mantra had stimulated some deep inner thoughts by him.

So, what is a mantra and why is a mantra important to every sales professional or entrepreneur? A mantra is a hymn, phrase, or slogan that one repeats to oneself over and over again so we are firmly grounded with great focus and purpose. I believe a mantra is very important in business because it keeps us zoned in on the present and future. It helps us concentrate on being the best businessperson we can be through robust and turbulent times.

Let's unpack my mantra… "Am I relevant? Do I add value?"

Relevance. In any sales or business environment, you always need to be in touch with your own maturation and meaning. Are you early, mid, or late cycle in your business vertical and/or specialty? This really matters in sales because it is important to always be on the ball, cracking open new accounts and business categories, or taking large pieces of business away from your competitors. Relevance means you are always comparing your productivity to the market in general and your immediate collegial environment. It asks whether you are a best-of-breed sales professional, sales manager, or product developer. It also means that you have to keep re-evaluating your monthly, quarterly, and yearly goals. You do this to make sure you are still very much running with the sales leaders within your company and sales vertical. Finally, and most importantly, it means you are constantly watching trends developing in your business and trying to anticipate how you can take advantage of these business gear shifts with new and long-standing corporate customers alike.

Value. In questioning the value you bring to the table every day, you are prodding yourself to look for new revenue sources for the company. You are also pushing yourself to take positive risks in thinking outside of the company's current revenue streams. Additionally, value speaks to the consistency and focus of your mindset around all elements of your work and revenue-generating responsibilities. There is one more element to value. It has to do with speaking the truth to your senior management team when they are doing well or heading down slippery slopes that could bring bad decision-making and revenue deterioration into play. I believe this last thought is the toughest. In a sales environment where we are all supposed to be smart at solving customer and revenue problems, few really want to hear from a dissenter.

Nevertheless, there you have it. Every day as I travelled to work, I thought about all of the above. Every day before I touched the handle of the front door of our offices, I always asked myself … "Am I relevant? Do I add value?"

Lessons Learned. Today, we live in a disruptive, ever-changing business environment of swinging door ownership, new management teams, and cultural shifts. My mantra might have been cold, but it kept me relevant and continuously adding value throughout my entire career. So, here's my question, "What will your corporate sales mantra be?"

PART V– SIX CORPORATE

NEGOTIATION STRATEGIES

45

CORPORATE SALES NEGOTIATION BUYER STRATEGIES

Our goal in this section of *The Bonus Round* is to help identify, name, and manage risk for six of the most essential negotiation strategies that buyers use in a corporate negotiation setting. By understanding these bargaining strategies, sellers will have a greater opportunity to react quicker to them. This allows us to weigh our options, neutralize their strategy, or call for a change in strategy to maximize our sales negotiation potential.

At Centroid Training, we love to teach negotiation strategy. These are six of our favourite easy-to-understand negotiation strategies. We see these strategies being used on sellers over and over again. Any of these strategies can be used by buyers singularly or in combination. When used in combination, these negotiation strategies become extra powerful. Sellers, stay alert.

To learn all the 25 Buyer and Seller negotiation strategies we teach at Centroid Training, invest in yourself and please buy a copy of ***Unlocking Yes, the Revised Edition***. It is the most muscular sales negotiation strategy book in the market today.

1. Buyer Creates a Bidding War, With an Account Review

This is a strong buyer negotiation strategy. It puts absolutely all sellers on notice that there is a tectonic move happening. The buyer risk is reasonably low with this negotiation strategy. Notwithstanding, if the buyer changes top suppliers, there is always a window of transition. Changes of systems are where big problems can, and often do, occur. Seller risk, though, is very high. This is when your navigational and allied relationships throughout the buyer company will be tested. It is a time to contact people throughout the buyer's organization to find out what you as a seller can do to save the account. Think; what is causing this account review? From a time-compression point of view, the sellers are on an hour glass clock. Every minute you do not act to save the account and identify the event that brought about the account review, your risk meter moves up.

Tip: If all else fails, have your company President call the buyer President directly. Chief Executives, generally, have a collegial approach to speaking directly to hidden, often game-changing, issues.

2. Buyer Creates a Share & Compare Quote Scheme

"Share & Compare" is one of my least favourite buyer strategies. It is a blunt instrument used by aggressive buyers who generally place little value on confidentiality and long-term relationships. The risk for the buyer is low in this environment with the exception of one key area: trust. How can a seller trust a buyer who is using another seller's confidential proposal as a leverage instrument? The risk to the seller is elevated in that, closing a deal with a buyer using this strategy means our seller proposal/deal is now expected to be public knowledge in the foreseeable future. Time compression is reasonably high. The seller will have to make a decision fairly quickly as to whether they want to pursue this business knowing the buyer could be using the same strategy with several of your competitors simultaneously.

This strategy is a con-game. Believe it or not, it has been used by large dollar volume corporate buyers when they feel they need to leverage a deal.

Tip: Visualize working with this customer several years ahead. What does the relationship look like in your mind? How much valuable information can you reasonably pass over to this customer? Do you take your best ideas to this customer? Do you treat this relationship as a commoditized strategic sell?

My counsel is to be very "Spartan" with releasing deep data to a customer who is utilizing a Share & Compare. Know that you are essentially buying the business with this customer. Be prepared for volatility in maintaining this sale, as it will always be on the auction block.

3. Split the Difference Strategy

The, "Split the Difference Strategy," is one of the most overused and most misunderstood negotiation strategies ever. There are entire business categories (think Real Estate) that use this negotiation strategy as a foundation. Therefore, as an outsider, if you don't want to play "split the difference," you are in many cases considered rude or uneducated. This last notion is anything but the truth.

The problem with the split the difference approach is that it usually benefits the negotiation partner initiating the strategy. Therefore, the risk is laid on the party receiving this negotiation strategy. One more thing, time-compression risk can be a big factor. Let me explain. Let's say you see a house for sale at $200,000 and you have a mortgage approval for exactly $180,000. You put an offer of $180,000 thinking the price you are offering is fair after reviewing the house prices in the neighbourhood and the condition of the home you are pursuing. The seller wanting to sell at full price says, "I will sell to you if we can split the difference in our valuations." If you accept this offer, the seller has convinced you to raise your bid by $10,000 or approximately 6% over what you thought was fair value for the house. My question is: why would anyone go into a negotiation knowing they will be expected, even cajoled, to raise their offer just to appear civil or in good form? Since we have no opportunity to raise more money, asking for the seller's chattels in the home is pointless.

Tip: If you are negotiating with someone and they say, "Come on, let's just split the difference", ask yourself, why would this negotiation partner want to do this? Who has the advantage in this scheme? Smart money says, go back and look at your backup plans. If the numbers don't make sense, go to your next plan or politely refuse the offer.

4. Poor Mouth, "We Have No Money" Strategy

If I have heard "poor mouth" once, I have heard "We have no money", as a strategy, a hundred times. This strategy is not limited to small businesses truly facing day-to-day survival. Just the opposite is true. Very successful mid-tier and even large corporations use the poor mouth strategy. When larger businesses use this negotiation strategy, it is premeditated and it could be cultural.

Be wary of "C Level" officers of businesses who want to probe for information and ask for advice about their problems. When you enquire about budget, the violins start to play in the background. One CEO, who ran a nationally branded company, wanted my help and went on to say he ran a rather small company. Also, he actually told me he couldn't say for sure that he had any budget. If the CEO does not know about his budget, we have a problem.

177

In larger corporations, the poor mouth, "we have no money" strategy is used citing limited departmental budgets and arguing that any funds that they do have must be stretched until their year-end.

Tip: When exposed to the poor mouth strategy, let your profitability and your cost modeling guide you. Don't get drawn in by all of the false theatrics. Remember, when we negotiate in good faith, we must be allowed to be profitable. Otherwise, we are being used.

5. The Growing List Strategy

With the "Growing List" Strategy,- we have to pay very close attention to professional corporate buyers who chip away at our profitability in a sales negotiation by insidiously adding pieces into a deal for which they have no intention of paying. In the "growing list" strategy, buyers gently nudge us to comply with requests for an upgrade here and a freebie there until the deal starts to feel a little lopsided.

These add-on requests can happen at the front of a deal or the back of a deal. I had one customer who would meet with me and pretend to be moving toward a deal. He would start to get into the details of the deal until important information was shared from our side that could well be considered billable information. He would pause for a moment and say something to the effect of, "Thank you for sharing, but don't bill me for that." He was using his leverage at the front end of the deal to extract extra value before we could even get a real idea how big the budget was. He was very adroit with this "growing list" strategy. Other buyers simply try to pressure us at the end of a deal while signing the deal. They continue the conversation with, "I know this means nothing to you, but could you please tuck in a couple of X, Y, & Zs as a show of good faith on your side?" By doing this, the buyer places us in an uncomfortable position. We either accept this "growing list" of items at no cost in his/her version of good faith, or it forces us to push back. This makes us look like a nickel-squeezing seller partner.

Tip: Make sure you keep a running total on the true value and cost of any "growing list" items added into a deal without expected payment. Make the corporate customer aware of the real value of these items. If the items are too costly, I recommend asking for something from the customer to justify this increased cost. In other words, see if you can get them to expand the pie a bit. You don't have to win the entire argument with this approach. You just want to make sure the customer knows you are looking for a collaborative business partner, one who realizes that you, as a seller, must be profitable. If the customer listens to you with some sense of empathy and adds a little more to their side of the deal, you know you have a great relationship in the making. If the customer shrugs you off as if their behaviour is normal and should be accepted, keep a really close eye on your costs. I recommend you limit your exposure to customers who treat you in this manner.

6. The Bonus Round Strategy

In my view, there was no one better at using the subtle nuances of time compression and time decompression than Steve Cosic, former Director of Media Procurement for the Hudson's Bay Company in Canada. Steve was a genius at buyer negotiation strategy.

Steve had a number of great proposals presented to him weekly by media suppliers. Each proposal presented would get his close scrutiny. More often than not, he would pause after what could be seen as a buying signal from him to many of us. This was all part of a crafty strategy that worked amazingly on unwitting corporate sellers.

Steve would just pause, wait, and start to mutter to himself or shuffle paper on his desk. He wouldn't fill the silence until the seller would say something such as, "Steve, you seem hesitant. What would it take to close this deal?" To which Steve would reply, "What do you have in mind?"

The seller would reveal one more value or discount-sweetener to the tabled proposal and Steve would often sign the deal.

Many years later, after leaving his role, Steve revealed to me that beautifully placed time delays and silence yielded tons more extra value and expenditure savings for his employer. Steve lovingly called that time-delay negotiation strategy, "The Bonus Round."

Tip: Sellers, you really have to do your homework on professional, seasoned corporate buyers. Buyers who have a huge selection of negotiation strategies to draw on are hard to predict. My recommendation is that when heading into an important negotiation with a big-time buyer, call those in your industry who have negotiated with this buyer. Find out their likes and dislikes, their values, their body language, tells, and their repeated bargaining strategy tendencies. There is no perfect defense in a buyer/seller relationship, but there are ways to reduce seller risk and price contagion.

STRATEGY SUMMARY

The six buyer negotiation strategies I have shared with you are being used by your customers on an hourly and daily basis. Therefore, it is in your best interest to sharpen your corporate sales negotiation game. You must learn to identify these strategies early in negotiations. Learn how to neutralize them or reroute them into a less competitive and more collaborative-based channel. What makes all of these strategies even more effective and compelling is that buyers are using these strategies by phone, email, Skype, and Zoom. This means that as a corporate seller, you are losing more and more face-time with your customers. This means you do not have the ability to read your negotiation partner's face and body movements, which are so critical to understanding how stressed or how serious they really are. It says to me that we must raise our sales negotiation game. We must do our best to pull game theory-based agreements toward more amicably based negotiations, where both parties are permitted to be profitable. We want strong, smart, relationship-based deals that stand the test of time.

My final tip is to read and re-read the strategy section of *The Bonus Round*. Commit to memory these strategies. The more you focus on sales negotiation strategy, the more successful and profitable you will be in all elements of your business and personal life. Finally, "Here's to negotiating wisely and profitably."

Patrick Tinney

PART VI – FINAL THOUGHTS

46

FINAL THOUGHTS: THE BONUS ROUND

Selling in a corporate setting is just plain challenging. As I mentioned earlier, there is big money to be made, but pressure is the price you pay to play. There is one more element that I have alluded to, but not entirely covered, and that is inter-company politics. Some in corporate sales are so focused on managing up that they lose sight of the mission. The mission is always to grow existing customers and bring new customers into our company fold.

When things became too political in the companies in which I worked, I always asked myself, "Is this issue part of our core mission? Does this mission make sense? Does this issue point toward true north? Or, does this issue smell like three-week-old dead fish?" Stay clear of issues that are going to harm your career. Furthermore, help those in need and stand up for those who are being taken advantage of. We can all do better. We can all help bring our sales brothers and sisters forward in a low self-interest manner. This is what it means to be professional.

Honestly, I wish there was more room in **The Bonus Round** for more great stories, business cases and examples of how to live your sales dreams. The good news is that I have written **Perpetual Hunger**, which is about top-drawer sales prospecting. I also wrote **Unlocking Yes, the Revised Edition**, which is about mind-bending, big time sales negotiations, and bursting with deep strategic approaches to closing monster deals. If you read all three of my books, you will have the sales panorama of sales prospecting, consultative selling, and sales negotiation at your finger-tips. These three books have always been meant to be bolted together. They are also meant to lift you and level you up. The truth is that sales learning is continuous. It must be continuous because the world demands our best. Technology, databases, artificial intelligence, and brilliant entrepreneurs will always push boundaries. This means sales must always push boundaries so that the sales panorama becomes even richer and more robust.

If you apply what I have offered you in my three sales books, you can sell anywhere. I mean that sincerely. I have 40+ years in active sales and I can tell you that great lessons do not get old. Integrity does not lose its luster. It means you care about your customers to the point that they become friends, not just a number. Honesty must be our gold standard. There will be days when both your honesty and integrity will be tested. Greed and high self-interest will be the villains. You will need to take long walks in the snow or along a beach to sort this out. Just remember, some day you will have to explain your career to your children and be their true north.

I would like to leave you with some challenges and goals. How are you going to live your sales dreams? How are you going to mentor and pay it forward in a charitable manner? Finally, how are you going to raise the level of professionalism in corporate sales? Answer these questions truthfully and you will constructively change the world for those around you and for those you serve as a top-drawer, corporate sales professional.

Finally, embrace empathy and compassion. Always show grace under fire.

Patrick Tinney

ACKNOWLEDGEMENTS

I cannot imagine writing a book in total isolation.

This list of wonderful people helped, pushed, pulled, cajoled, and cheered me on as I discovered *The Bonus Round*

Please accept my gratitude:

Doug Brown

Deb Calvert

Mladenka Cosic

Randy Craig

Drew Harris

Mark Hunter

Chris Kata

Braden Marshall

James Muir

Milan Topolovec

and Raj Narula…

to mention a few.

I want to extend a special thank you to my amazing family, who put up with my relentless march forward.

Patrick Tinney

A special thank you goes to my grammar coach Margret Hall. Margret has the eyes of an eagle.

A profound thank you goes to Glenn Marshall and the Greening Marketing team for their expert knowledge on creative and cover design. They are brilliant advertising agency professionals executing on what they do best.

Finally, here's to my corporate sales brothers and sisters who lift above their belt weight.

INDEX

D

E

F

G

H

I

K

L

M

N

O

P

Q

R

NOTES

Patrick Tinney

NOTES

NOTES

Patrick Tinney

NOTES

About the Author

Build the skills that matter through

WORKSHOPS

KEYNOTES

BUSINESS & PITCH COACHING

CONSULTATIONS

Patrick Tinney is an experienced business sales professional who shares his real life, real deals experience. Patrick lives and practices the principles of sales prospecting, consultative selling, and sales negotiation addressed in his writings. Business leaders count on Patrick's unwavering commitment to their success.

Patrick Tinney

Centroid Training & Marketing

www.centroidmarketing.com

Helping businesses make and save money.

Bus: (705) 657-2518 Mobile: (416) 617-3271

Email: patrick@centroidmarketing.com

Twitter: #Centroideals

LinkedIn: Patrick Tinney

Patrick Tinney's other sales and negotiation books are available at Chapters.ca and Amazon.com world-wide!